MATH Trailblazers®

A BALANCED MATHEMATICS PROGRAM INTEGRATING SCIENCE AND LANGUAGE ARTS

Facts Resource Guide

×	0	1	2	3	4	5	6	7	8	9	10
0	0	0	0	0	0	0	0	0	0	0	0
1	0	1	2	3	4	5	6	7	8	9	10
2	0	2	4	6	8	10	12	14	16	18	20
3	0	3	6	9	12	15	18	21	24	27	30
4	0	4	8	12	16	20	24	28	32	36	40
5	0	5	10	15	20	25	30	35	40	45	50
6	0	6	12	18	24	30	36	42	48	54	60
7	0	7	14	21	28	35	42	49	56	63	70
8	0	8	16	24	32	40	48	56	64	72	80
9	0	9	18	27	36	45	54	63	72	81	90
10	0	10	20	30	40	50	60	70	80	90	100

THIRD EDITION

KENDALL/HUNT PUBLISHING COMPANY
4050 Westmark Drive   Dubuque, Iowa 52002

A TIMS® Curriculum
University of Illinois at Chicago

UIC The University of Illinois
at Chicago

The original edition was based on work supported by the National Science Foundation under grant
No. MDR 9050226 and the University of Illinois at Chicago. Any opinions, findings, and conclusions
or recommendations expressed in this publication are those of the author(s) and do not necessarily
reflect the views of the granting agencies.

Grade 5 Acknowledgments

Teaching Integrated Mathematics and Science (TIMS) Project Directors

Philip Wagreich, Principal Investigator
Joan L. Bieler
Howard Goldberg (emeritus)
Catherine Randall Kelso

Director

Third Edition — Joan L. Bieler

Curriculum Developers

Third Edition

Lindy M. Chambers-Boucher	Philip Wagreich
Janet Simpson Beissinger	

Contributors

Third Edition

Eileen Wynn Ball	Sandy Niemiera
Jenny Bay-Williams	Christina Nugent
Ava Chatterjee-Belisle	Janet M. Parsons
Elizabeth Colligan	Leona Peters
Marty Gartzman	Catherine Reed
Carol Inzerillo	

Editorial and Production Staff

Third Edition

Kathleen R. Anderson	Christina Clemons
Lindy M. Chambers-Boucher	Anne Roby

TIMS Professional Developers

Barbara Crum	Cheryl Kneubuhler
Catherine Ditto	Lisa Mackey
Pamela Guyton	Linda Miceli

TIMS Director of Media Services

Henrique Cirne-Lima

TIMS Research Staff

Stacy Brown	Catherine Ditto
Reality Canty	Kathleen Pitvorec
Alison Castro	Catherine Randall Kelso

TIMS Administrative Staff

Eve Ali Boles	Enrique Puente
Kathleen R. Anderson	Alice VanSlyke
Nida Khan	

Director

Second Edition — Catherine Randall Kelso

Curriculum Developers

Second Edition

Lindy M. Chambers-Boucher
Elizabeth Colligan
Marty Gartzman
Carol Inzerillo
Catherine Randall Kelso

Jennifer Mundt Leimberer
Georganne E. Marsh
Leona Peters
Philip Wagreich

Editorial and Production Staff

Second Edition

Kathleen R. Anderson
Ai-Ai C. Cojuangco
Andrada Costoiu
Erika Larsen

Georganne E. Marsh
Cosmina Menghes
Anne Roby

Principal Investigators

First Edition

Philip Wagreich

Howard Goldberg

Senior Curriculum Developers

First Edition

Janet Simpson Beissinger
Joan L. Bieler
Astrida Cirulis
Marty Gartzman
Howard Goldberg

Carol Inzerillo
Andy Isaacs
Catherine Randall Kelso
Leona Peters
Philip Wagreich

Curriculum Developers

First Edition

Janice C. Banasiak
Lynne Beauprez
Andy Carter
Lindy M. Chambers-Boucher
Kathryn Chval
Diane Czerwinski

Jenny Knight
Sandy Niemiera
Janice Ozima
Polly Tangora
Paul Trafton

Illustrator

First Edition

Kris Dresen

Editorial and Production Staff

First Edition

Glenda L. Genio-Terrado
Mini Joseph
Lynette Morgenthaler

Sarah Nelson
Birute Petrauskas
Anne Roby

Research Consultant

First Edition

Andy Isaacs

Mathematics Education Consultant

First Edition

Paul Trafton

National Advisory Committee

First Edition

Carl Berger
Tom Berger
Hugh Burkhart
Donald Chambers
Naomi Fisher
Glenda Lappan

Mary Lindquist
Eugene Maier
Lourdes Monteagudo
Elizabeth Phillips
Thomas Post

Grade 5 — Table of Contents

Math Trailblazers® includes a comprehensive, research-based program for teaching basic math facts. This program is carefully integrated into the lessons and Daily Practice and Problems (DPP) of each grade and the Home Practice in Grades 3–5. The *Grade 5 Facts Resource Guide* is a compilation of much of the math facts materials for fifth grade. These include math facts lessons, relevant DPP items, Home Practice parts, flash cards, *Facts I Know* charts, the TIMS Tutor: *Math Facts,* and information for parents about the *Math Trailblazers* math facts philosophy.

Classrooms that stay close to the suggested pacing schedule for teaching lessons will have little difficulty implementing the complete math facts program without this guide. A pacing schedule is in the *Unit Resource Guide* and the Grade 5 Overview section in the *Teacher Implementation Guide*. In those classrooms, teachers can simply use the math facts materials built into the lessons, Daily Practice and Problems, and Home Practice. However, because the math facts program is closely linked to the recommended schedule for teaching lessons, classrooms that differ significantly from the suggested pacing of units will need to make special accommodations to ensure that students receive a consistent program of math facts practice and assessment throughout the year. This manual will assist teachers with that process.

All of the materials included in the *Grade 5 Facts Resource Guide* are located elsewhere in *Math Trailblazers*. Wherever appropriate, we will include a reference to an item's location in other *Math Trailblazers* components.

A major goal of *Math Trailblazers* is to prepare students to compute accurately, flexibly, and appropriately in all situations. Standard topics in arithmetic—acquisition of basic math facts and fluency with whole-number operations—are covered extensively.

In developing our program for the math facts, we sought a careful balance between strategies and drill. This approach is based on a large body of research and advocated by the National Council of Teachers of Mathematics (NCTM) *Principles and Standards for School Mathematics* and by the National Research Council in *Adding It Up: Helping Children Learn Mathematics*. The research indicates that the methods used in the *Math Trailblazers* math facts program lead to more effective learning and better retention of the math facts and also help develop essential math skills.

For a detailed discussion of the math facts program in *Math Trailblazers,* see Section 3 TIMS Tutor: *Math Facts.* See also Section 2 *Information for Parents: Math Facts Philosophy.*

What Is the *Math Trailblazers* Facts Resource Guide?

Introduction to the Math Facts in *Math Trailblazers*

The following table describes the development of math facts and whole number operations in *Math Trailblazers*. The shaded portions of the table highlight development of the math facts program in each grade. Expectations for fluency with math facts are indicated in bold. The white portions of the table highlight development of the whole-number operations.

Grade	Addition	Subtraction	Multiplication	Division
K	Introduce concepts through problem solving and use of manipulatives.			
1	Develop strategies for addition facts. Solve addition problems in context.	Develop strategies for subtraction facts. Solve subtraction problems in context.	Develop concepts through problem solving and use of manipulatives.	
2	Continue use of addition facts in problems. Continue use of strategies for addition facts. **Assess for fluency with addition facts.** Continue solving addition problems in context. Introduce procedures for multidigit addition using manipulatives and paper and pencil.	Continue use of subtraction facts in problems. Continue use of strategies for subtraction facts. **Assess for fluency with subtraction facts.** Continue solving subtraction problems in context. Introduce procedures for multidigit subtraction using manipulatives and paper and pencil.	Continue concept development through problem solving and use of manipulatives.	
3	Diagnose and remediate with addition facts as needed. Develop procedures for multidigit addition using manipulatives and paper and pencil. Practice and apply multidigit addition in varied contexts.	Maintain fluency with subtraction facts through review and assessment. Develop procedures for multidigit subtraction using manipulatives and paper and pencil. Practice and apply multidigit subtraction in varied contexts.	Continue use of multiplication facts in problems. Develop strategies for multiplication facts. **Assess for fluency with multiplication facts.** Solve multiplication problems in context. Introduce paper-and-pencil multiplication of one digit by two digits.	Continue use of division facts in problems. Develop strategies for division facts. Continue concept development. Solve division problems in context.
4	Diagnose and remediate with addition facts as needed. Practice and apply multidigit addition in varied contexts. Review paper-and-pencil procedures for multidigit addition.	Diagnose and remediate with subtraction facts as needed. Practice and apply multidigit subtraction in varied contexts. Review paper-and-pencil procedures for multidigit subtraction.	Maintain fluency with multiplication facts through review and assessment. Develop procedures for multiplication using manipulatives and paper and pencil (1-digit and 2-digit multipliers). Practice and apply multiplication in varied contexts.	Continue use of division facts in problems. Continue development of strategies for division facts. **Assess for fluency with division facts.** Solve division problems in context. Develop procedures for division using manipulatives and paper and pencil (1-digit divisors).
5	Diagnose and remediate with addition facts as needed. Practice and apply multidigit addition in varied contexts.	Diagnose and remediate with subtraction facts as needed. Practice and apply multidigit subtraction in varied contexts.	Maintain fluency with multiplication facts through review and assessment. Review paper-and-pencil procedures. Practice and apply multiplication in varied contexts.	Maintain fluency with division facts through review and assessment. Develop paper-and-pencil procedures with one- and two-digit divisors. Practice and apply division in varied contexts.

Table 1: *Math Facts and Whole-Number Operations Overview*

Addition and Subtraction Diagnosis and Review

Most work with math facts in Grade 5 focuses on reviewing and assessing the multiplication and division facts. However, Unit 1 begins with an opportunity to assess students' fluency with the addition and subtraction facts. Those students who exhibit reasonable fluency with the addition and subtraction facts will continue to practice these facts throughout the year in labs, activities, and games, and as they solve items in the DPP and Home Practice. Review is provided for students who still lack fluency with the addition and subtraction facts.

The Addition and Subtraction Math Facts Review in Section 8 provides practice activities for students who require further work with addition and subtraction math facts. Students can use the suggested activities, games, and flash cards at home with family members. Distribute this work over time, rather than giving it all at once. While working with the addition and subtraction facts, students should continue with the rest of the class on the review of multiplication and division facts in the Daily Practice and Problems, Home Practice, and other lessons. They can use strategies, manipulatives, and calculators as they solve problems in class or at home.

Multiplication and Division Review and Assessment

A systematic review of the multiplication and division facts begins in Unit 2. The multiplication and division facts are divided into groups similar to the groups students studied in Grades 3 and 4.

The distribution for the review of multiplication and division math facts in Grade 5 is outlined in Table 2. Formal assessments of the facts for each group are included in the DPP in Units 2–7, with a test on all facts given in Unit 8. Each group is reviewed in Units 9–16 without additional formal assessments.

Unit	Math Facts Groups
1	Addition and Subtraction Assessment
2	5s and 10s
3	2s and 3s
4	Square Numbers
5	9s
6	Last Six Facts (4×6, 4×7, 4×8, 6×7, 6×8, 7×8)
7	Review all facts.
8	Assess all facts.
9*	5s and 10s
10*	2s and Square Numbers
11*	3s and 9s
12*	Last Six Facts (4×6, 4×7, 4×8, 6×7, 6×8, 7×8)
13*	2s, 5s, 10s, and Square Numbers
14*	3s, 9s, and Last Six Facts
15*	Review all facts.
16*	Review all facts.

*Units 9–16 do not include formal, paper-and-pencil assessments of the fact groups.

Table 2: *Math Facts Groups*

Launching the Study of the Multiplication and Division Facts. Unit 2 Lesson 2 *Facts I Know* sets up the math facts strand in Grade 5, beginning with the fives and tens.

In Part 1 of Lesson 2:

- Students quiz each other on the multiplication facts for the fives and tens. They use *Triangle Flash Cards* to assess themselves on the facts. They sort the cards into three piles: those they can answer quickly; those they can figure out with a strategy; and those they need to learn.

- They begin a record of their current progress with the multiplication facts for the fives and tens by using a self-assessment page called the *Multiplication Facts I Know* chart. They circle the multiplication facts they know and can answer quickly. The chart is updated throughout Units 2–8.

In Part 2 of Lesson 2:

- Students review the fact families for the fives and tens (e.g., $5 \times 3 = 15$, $3 \times 5 = 15$, $15 \div 3 = 5$, and $15 \div 5 = 3$).

- They practice the multiplication and division facts they need to study for the fives and tens.

In Part 3 of Lesson 2:

- Students sort the flash cards for the fives and tens again, this time focusing on the division facts.

- They circle the division facts they know and can answer quickly on *Division Facts I Know* charts, which they update throughout Units 2–8.

After completing Lesson 2, students continue to practice the facts for the fives and tens by completing various Daily Practice and Problems (DPP) items. Near the end of the unit, a DPP item includes a quiz on the fives and tens. Students take the quiz and update their *Multiplication* and *Division Facts I Know* charts.

Math Facts in the Daily Practice and Problems for Units 3–16. Students practice the multiplication and division facts as they solve problems in labs, activities, and games. However, the systematic practice and assessment of the math facts takes place primarily in the DPP. The study of the math facts in the DPP for Units 3–6 parallels the process in Unit 2:

1. A DPP item instructs students to quiz each other on a group of multiplication facts using the *Triangle Flash Cards.* Students sort the cards into three piles as described above. They update their *Multiplication Facts I Know* charts.

2. Additional DPP items provide practice with the multiplication and division fact families for a particular group.

3. A DPP item instructs students to sort the flash cards again, focusing on the division facts. Students update their *Division Facts I Know* charts.

4. A final DPP item includes a quiz that assesses students on a mixture of multiplication and division facts for a particular group. Students take the quiz and update their *Multiplication* and *Division Facts I Know* charts.

The DPP for Units 7 and 8 review all five groups of facts. As students complete these items, they update their *Multiplication* and *Division Facts I Know* charts. A final DPP item in Unit 8 includes an inventory test on multiplication and division facts from all five groups. The test helps teachers and students assess which facts they know and which facts they still need to learn. This marks the end of the formal assessment program for the math facts in *Math Trailblazers.*

The DPP in Units 9–16 includes additional math facts review, especially of the division facts. These will provide further opportunities for students to strengthen their fluency with the math facts. Students can use their *Triangle Flash Cards* to practice the multiplication and division facts they have not circled on their *Facts I Know* charts.

Using the *Facts Resource Guide*

As indicated above, the *Math Trailblazers* program for teaching math facts in Grade 5 is based on a distributed study of the facts, located largely in the DPP for each unit. The orderly distribution of the facts will be disrupted if the pacing of the program is altered from the recommended schedule. The *Grade 5 Facts Resource Guide* provides an alternative schedule for the study and assessment of math facts for teachers who fall significantly behind the estimated number of class sessions assigned per unit. (If you do not fall behind the recommended schedule, you do not need to use the *Grade 5 Facts Resource Guide*—simply follow the math facts program in the units.)

The *Grade 5 Facts Resource Guide* translates the math facts program into a week-by-week calendar that roughly approximates the schedule for studying the math facts that a class would follow if they remain close to the designated schedule for *Math Trailblazers* lessons. (See the Math Facts Calendar in Section 4.) In this manner, students will review all the math facts for their particular grade even if they do not complete all the units for the year.

This program is based on research that shows that students learn the facts better using a strategies-based approach accompanied by distributed practice of small groups of facts. Therefore, we strongly recommend against using the math facts program in a shorter amount of time. The program can be tailored to the needs of individual students using the *Multiplication* and *Division Facts I Know* charts. Those students who know the facts based on the *Triangle Flash Cards* self-assessment will not need much practice. Other students will find they only need to study one or two facts in a group. Still others will need to work on more facts, using the flash cards and games at home.

It is important to note that in *Math Trailblazers* much of the work for gaining fluency with math facts arises naturally in the problem-solving activities completed in class and for homework. Thus, the math facts items included in the *Grade 5 Facts Resource Guide* do not reflect the full scope of the math facts program in the *Math Trailblazers* curriculum.

Resources

Isaacs, A.C., and W.M. Carroll. "Strategies for Basic Facts Instruction." *Teaching Children Mathematics,* 5 May, pp. 508–15, 1999.

National Research Council. "Developing Proficiency with Whole Numbers." In *Adding It Up: Helping Children Learn Mathematics,* J. Kilpatrick, J. Swafford, and B. Findell, eds. National Academy Press, Washington, DC, 2001.

Principles and Standards for School Mathematics. National Council of Teachers of Mathematics, Reston, VA, 2000.

Thornton, C.A. "Strategies for the Basic Facts." In J.N. Payne (ed.), *Mathematics for the Young Child.* National Council of Teachers of Mathematics, Reston, VA, 1990.

To inform parents about the curriculum's goals and philosophy of learning and assessing the math facts, send home a copy of the *Grade 5 Math Facts Philosophy* that immediately follows. This document is also available in the Unit 2 *Unit Resource Guide* immediately following the Background and on the *Teacher Resource CD.*

Information for Parents
Grade 5 Math Facts Philosophy

The goal of the math facts strand in *Math Trailblazers* is for students to learn the basic facts efficiently, gain fluency with their use, and retain that fluency over time. In fifth grade, students review the multiplication and division facts.

A large body of research supports an approach in which students develop strategies for figuring out the facts rather than relying solely on rote memorization. This not only leads to more effective learning and better retention, but also to development of mental math skills useful throughout life. Therefore, the teaching and assessment of the basic facts in *Math Trailblazers* is characterized by the following elements:

Use of Strategies. In earlier grades, students first approached the basic facts as problems to be solved rather than as facts to be memorized. In all grades we encourage the use of strategies to find facts and de-emphasize rote memorization. Thus students become confident they can find answers to fact problems they do not immediately recall. In this way, students learn that math is more than memorizing facts and rules which "you either get or you don't."

Distributed Review of the Facts. Students study small groups of facts that can be found using similar strategies. In fifth grade, the multiplication and division facts are divided into five groups. During the first semester students review these facts, one group at a time. They practice both the multiplication and division facts in each group. Students use flash cards to review groups of facts at home. Using this systematic approach, they build upon the fluency with the multiplication and the division facts gained in fourth grade.

Practice in Context. Students also review the facts as they use them to solve problems in the labs, activities, and games.

Appropriate Assessment. Students are regularly assessed to determine whether they can find answers to fact problems quickly and accurately and whether they can retain this skill over time. A short quiz follows the study and review of each group of facts. Each student records his or her progress on "Facts I Know" charts and determines the facts he or she still needs to study.

Facts Will Not Act as Gatekeepers. Students are not prevented from learning more complex mathematics because they cannot perform well on fact tests. Use of strategies, calculators, and printed multiplication tables allows students to continue to work on interesting problems and experiments while they are learning the facts.

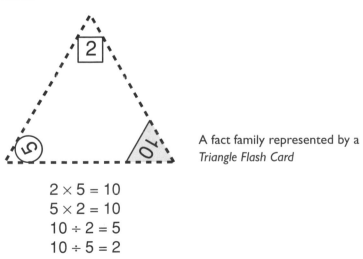

A fact family represented by a *Triangle Flash Card*

$2 \times 5 = 10$
$5 \times 2 = 10$
$10 \div 2 = 5$
$10 \div 5 = 2$

Información para los padres

La filosofía de los conceptos matemáticos básicos en 5to. grado

El objetivo de enseñanza de los conceptos matemáticos básicos en Math Trailblazers es que los estudiantes aprendan los conceptos básicos eficazmente, logren el dominio de estos conceptos y mantengan ese dominio con el paso del tiempo. En 5to grado, los estudiantes repasan las tablas de multiplicación y división.

La investigación realizada respalda la aplicación de un enfoque en el que los estudiantes desarrollan estrategias para resolver los problemas de conceptos básicos en lugar de aprenderlas de memoria. Esto no sólo permite un aprendizaje más eficaz y una mejor retención, sino que también desarrolla habilidades matemáticas mentales que serán útiles durante toda la vida. Por lo tanto, la enseñanza y la evaluación de los conceptos básicos en *Math Trailblazers* se caracteriza por los siguientes elementos:

El uso de estrategias. Los estudiantes enfocan primero a los conceptos básicos como problemas para resolver en lugar de tablas para memorizar. En todos los grados, alentamos el uso de estrategias para hallar soluciones y damos menos énfasis en aprender de memoria. De este modo, los estudiantes tienen más confianza de poder hallar las soluciones de problemas de cuales no se acuerdan. De esta manera, los estudiantes aprenden que las matemáticas son más que tablas y reglas memorizadas que un estudiante "sabe o no sabe".

Repaso gradual de los conceptos básicos. Los estudiantes estudian pequeños grupos de conceptos básicos que pueden hallarse usando estrategias similares. En quinto grado, las tablas de multiplicación y división se dividen en cinco grupos. Durante el primer semestre, los estudiantes repasan estos conceptos básicos, un grupo por vez. Los estudiantes practican tanto las tablas de multiplicación como las divisiones relacionadas en cada grupo. Los estudiantes usan tarjetas para practicar los grupos de conceptos básicos en casa. Usando este enfoque sistemático, se refuerza el dominio de las tablas de multiplicación y división adquirido en cuarto grado.

Práctica en contexto. Los estudiantes también repasan los conceptos básicos cuando los usan en experiencias de laboratorio, actividades y juegos.

Evaluación apropiada. Evaluamos a los estudiantes habitualmente para determinar si pueden hallar respuestas rápidas y correctas a problemas que involucran los conceptos básicos, y para determinar si pueden retener esta habilidad con el paso del tiempo. Los estudiantes deben completar un examen corto después de estudiar y repasar cada grupo de conceptos básicos. Cada estudiante registra su progreso en tablas tituladas "Las tablas las conozco" y determina qué tablas necesita estudiar todavía.

El nivel de dominio de los conceptos básicos no impedirá el aprendizaje. Los estudiantes seguirán aprendiendo conceptos matemáticos más complejos aunque no les vaya bien en los exámenes sobre los conceptos básicos. El uso de estrategias, calculadoras y tablas de multiplicación impresas les permite continuar trabajando en problemas y experimentos interesantes mientras aprenden los conceptos básicos.

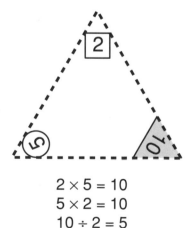

$$2 \times 5 = 10$$
$$5 \times 2 = 10$$
$$10 \div 2 = 5$$
$$10 \div 5 = 2$$

Los conceptos relacionados representados por una tarjeta triangular.

The TIMS Tutor: *Math Facts* provides an in-depth exploration of the math facts concepts and ideas behind the math facts strand in *Math Trailblazers*. This document also appears in the *Teacher Implementation Guide*.

Students need to learn the math facts. Estimation, mental arithmetic, checking the reasonableness of results, and paper-and-pencil calculations require the ability to give quick, accurate responses when using basic facts. The question is not if students should learn the math facts, but how. Which teaching methods are most efficient and effective? To answer this question, we as authors of *Math Trailblazers* drew upon educational research and our own classroom experiences to develop a comprehensive plan for teaching the math facts.

Philosophy

The goal of the *Math Trailblazers* math facts strand is for students to learn the basic facts efficiently, gain fluency with their use, and retain that fluency over time. A large body of research supports an approach that is built on a foundation of work with strategies and concepts. This not only leads to more effective learning and better retention, but also to development of mental math skills. Therefore, the teaching and assessment of the basic facts in *Math Trailblazers* is characterized by the following elements:

- *Early emphasis on problem solving.* Students first approach the basic facts as problems to solve rather than as facts to memorize. Students invent their own strategies to solve these problems or learn appropriate strategies from others through class discussion. Students' natural strategies, especially counting strategies, are explicitly encouraged. In this way, students learn that math is more than memorizing facts and rules that "you either get or you don't."

- *De-emphasis of rote work.* Fluency with the math facts is an important component of any student's mathematical learning. Research shows that overemphasizing memorization and frequent administration of timed tests are counterproductive. Both can produce undesirable results (Isaacs and Carroll, 1999; Van de Walle, 2001; National Research Council, 2001). We encourage the use of strategies to find facts, so students become confident they can find answers to fact problems they do not immediately recall.

- *Gradual and systematic introduction of facts.* Students study the facts in small groups they solve using similar strategies. Students first work on simple strategies for easy facts and then progress to more sophisticated strategies and harder facts. By the end of the process, they gain fluency with all required facts.

- *Ongoing practice.* Work on the math facts is distributed throughout the curriculum, especially in the Daily Practice and Problems (DPP), Home Practice, and games. This practice for fluency, however, takes place only after students have a conceptual understanding of the operations and have achieved proficiency with strategies for solving basic fact problems. Delaying practice in this way means that less practice is required to achieve fluency.

- *Appropriate assessment.* Teachers assess students' knowledge of the facts through observations as they work on activities, labs, and games as well as through the appropriate use of written tests and quizzes. Beginning in first grade, periodic, short quizzes in the DPP naturally follow the study of small groups of facts organized around specific strategies. As self-assessment in Grades 3–5, students record their progress on *Facts I Know* charts and determine which facts they need to study. Inventory tests of all facts for each operation are used sparingly in Grades 2–5 (no more than twice per year) to assess students' progress with fact fluency. The goal of the math facts assessment program is to determine the degree to which students can find answers to fact problems quickly and accurately and whether they can retain this skill over time.
- *Multiyear approach.* In Grades 1 and 2, *Math Trailblazers* emphasizes strategies that lead to fluency with the addition and subtraction facts. In Grade 3, students gain fluency with the multiplication facts while reviewing the addition and subtraction facts. In Grade 4, students achieve fluency with the division facts and verify fluency with the multiplication facts. In Grade 5, the multiplication and division facts are systematically reviewed and assessed.
- *Facts are not gatekeepers.* Students are not prevented from learning more complex mathematics because they do not perform well on fact tests. Use of strategies, calculators, and other math tools (e.g., manipulatives, hundred charts, printed multiplication tables) allows students to continue to work on interesting problems while still learning the facts.

The following goals for the math facts are consistent with the recommendations in the National Council of Teachers of Mathematics *Principles and Standards for School Mathematics:*

- In kindergarten, students use manipulatives and invent their own strategies to solve addition and subtraction problems.
- By the end of first grade, all students can solve all basic addition and subtraction problems using some strategy. Fluency is not emphasized; strategies are. Some work with beginning concepts of multiplication takes place.
- In second grade, learning efficient strategies for addition and especially subtraction continues to be emphasized. Work with multiplication concepts continues. By the end of the year, students are expected to demonstrate fluency with all the addition and subtraction facts.
- In third grade, students review the subtraction facts. They develop efficient strategies for learning the multiplication facts and demonstrate fluency with the multiplication facts.
- In fourth grade, students review the multiplication facts and develop strategies for the division facts. By the end of year, we expect fluency with all the division facts.
- In fifth grade, students review the multiplication and division facts and are expected to maintain fluency with all the facts.

Expectations by Grade Level

This is summarized in the following chart:

Grade	Addition	Subtraction	Multiplication	Division
K	• invented strategies	• invented strategies		
1	• strategies	• strategies		
2	• strategies • practice leading to fluency	• strategies • practice leading to fluency		
3	• review and practice	• review and practice	• strategies • practice leading to fluency	
4	• assessment and remediation as required	• assessment and remediation as required	• review and practice	• strategies • practice leading to fluency
5	• assessment and remediation as required	• assessment and remediation as required	• review and practice	• review and practice

Table 1: *Math Facts Scope and Sequence*

Strategies for Learning the Facts

Students are encouraged to learn the math facts by first employing a variety of strategies. Concepts and skills are learned more easily and are retained longer if they are meaningful. By first concentrating on concepts and strategies, we increase retention and reduce the amount of time necessary for rote memorization. Researchers note that over time, students develop techniques that are increasingly sophisticated and efficient. Experience with the strategies provides a basis for understanding the operation involved and for gaining fluency with the facts. In this section, we describe possible strategies for learning the addition, subtraction, multiplication, and division facts. The strategies for each operation are listed roughly in order of increasing sophistication.

Strategies for Addition Facts

Common strategies include counting all, counting on, doubles, making or using 10, and reasoning from known facts.

Counting All

This is a particularly straightforward strategy. For example, to solve 7 + 8, the student gets 7 of something and 8 of something and counts how many there are altogether. The "something" could be beans or chips or marks on paper. In any case, the student counts all the objects to find the sum. This is perhaps not a very efficient method, but it is effective, especially for small numbers, and is usually well understood by the student.

Counting On

This is a natural strategy, particularly for adding 1, 2, or 3. Counters such as beans or chips may or may not be used. As an example, consider $8 + 3$. The student gets 8 beans, and then 3 more, but instead of counting the first 8 again, she simply counts the 3 added beans: "9, 10, 11."

Even if counters are not used, finger gestures can help keep track of how many more have been counted on. For example, to solve $8 + 3$, the student counts "9, 10, 11," holding up a finger each time a number word is said; when three fingers are up, the last word said is the answer.

Doubles

Facts such as $4 + 4 = 8$ are easier to remember than facts with two different addends. Some visual imagery can help, too: two hands for $5 + 5$, a carton of eggs for $6 + 6$, a calendar for $7 + 7$, and so on.

Making a 10

Facts with a sum of 10, such as $7 + 3$ and $6 + 4$, are also easier to remember than other facts. Ten frames can create visual images of making a 10. For example, 8 is shown in a ten frame like the one in Figure 1:

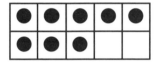

Figure 1: *A ten frame*

This visual imagery helps students remember, for example, that $8 + 2 = 10$.

Using a 10

Students who are comfortable partitioning and combining small numbers can use that knowledge to find the sums of larger numbers. In particular, there are many strategies that involve using the number 10. For example, to find $9 + 7$, we can decompose 7 into $1 + 6$ and then $9 + 7 = 9 + 1 + 6 = 10 + 6 = 16$. Similarly, $8 + 7 = 8 + 2 + 5 = 10 + 5 = 15$.

Reasoning from Known Facts

If you know what $7 + 7$ is, then $7 + 8$ is not much harder: it's just 1 more. So, the "near doubles" can be derived from knowing the doubles.

Strategies for Subtraction Facts

Common strategies for subtraction include using counters, counting up, counting back, using 10, and reasoning from related addition and subtraction facts.

Using Counters

This method models the problem with counters like beans or chips. For example, to solve $8 - 3$, the student gets 8 beans, removes 3 beans, and counts the remaining beans to find the difference. As with using the addition strategy "counting all," this relatively straightforward strategy may not be efficient but it has the great advantage that students usually understand it well.

Counting Up

The student starts at the lower number and counts on to the higher number, perhaps using fingers to keep track of how many numbers are counted. For example, to solve $8 - 5$, the student wants to know how to get from 5 to 8 and counts up 3 numbers: 6, 7, 8. So, $8 - 5 = 3$.

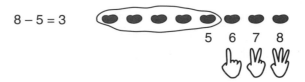

Figure 2: *Counting up*

Counting Back

Counting back works best for subtracting 1, 2, or 3. For larger numbers, it is probably best to count up. For example, to solve $9 - 2$, the student counts back 2 numbers: 8, 7. So, $9 - 2 = 7$.

$$9 - 2 = 7 \qquad 9 \quad 8 \quad 7$$

Figure 3: *Counting back*

Using a 10

Students follow the pattern they find when subtracting 10, e.g., $17 - 10 = 7$ and $13 - 10 = 3$, to learn close facts, e.g., $17 - 9 = 8$ and $13 - 9 = 4$. Since $17 - 9$ will be 1 more than $17 - 10$, they can reason that the answer will be 8, or $7 + 1$.

Making a 10

Knowing the addition facts that have a sum of 10, e.g., $6 + 4 = 10$, can be helpful in finding differences from 10, e.g., $10 - 6 = 4$ and $10 - 4 = 6$. Students can use ten frames to visualize these problems as in Figure 4. These facts can then also be used to find close facts, such as $11 - 4 = 7$.

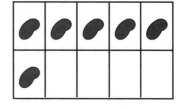

$$10 - 4 = 6$$

Figure 4: *Using a ten frame*

Using Doubles

Students can use the addition doubles, e.g., $8 + 8 = 16$ and $6 + 6 = 12$, to learn the subtraction "half-doubles" as well: $16 - 8 = 8$ and $12 - 6 = 6$. They can then use these facts to figure out close facts, such as $13 - 6 = 7$ and $15 - 8 = 7$.

Reasoning from Related Addition and Subtraction Facts

Knowing that $8 + 7 = 15$ would seem to be of some help in solving $15 - 7$. Unfortunately, however, knowing related addition facts may not be so helpful to younger or less mathematically mature students. Nevertheless, reasoning from known facts is a powerful strategy for those who can apply it and should be encouraged.

Strategies for Multiplication Facts

Common strategies for multiplication include skip counting, counting up or down from a known fact, doubling, breaking a product into the sum of known products, and using patterns.

Skip Counting

Students begin skip counting and solving problems informally that involve multiplicative situations in first grade. By the time they begin formal work with the multiplication facts in third grade, they should be fairly proficient with skip counting. This strategy is particularly useful for facts such as the 2s, 3s, 5s, and 10s, for which skip counting is easy.

Counting Up or Down from a Known Fact

This strategy involves skip counting forwards once or twice from a known fact. For example, if children know that 5×5 is 25, then they can use this to solve 6×5 (5 more) or 4×5 (5 less). Some children use this for harder facts. For 7×6, they can use the fact that $5 \times 6 = 30$ as a starting point and then count on by sixes to 42.

Doubling

Some children use doubling relationships to help them with multiplication facts involving 4, 6, and 8. For example, 4×7 is twice as much as 2×7. Since $2 \times 7 = 14$, it follows that 4×7 is 28. Since 3×8 is 24, it follows that 6×8 is 48.

Breaking a Product into the Sum of Known Products

A fact like 7×8 can be broken into the sum $5 \times 8 + 2 \times 8$ since $7 = 5 + 2$. See Figure 5. The previous two strategies are special cases of this more general strategy.

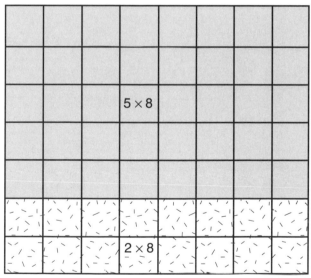

$$7 \times 8 =$$
$$5 \times 8 + 2 \times 8 =$$
$$40 + 16 = 56$$

Figure 5: *Breaking up 7 × 8*

Patterns

A. Perhaps the best-known examples of patterns are the nines patterns:

   1. When the nines products are listed in a column, as shown below, it is easy to see that the digits in the tens place count up by one (0, 1, 2, 3, . . .) and that the digits in the ones place count down by one (9, 8, 7, . . .).

     9
    18
    27
    36
    45
    54
    63
    72
    81

   2. The sums of the two digits in each of the nines products above are all equal to nine. For example, the sum of the digits in 36 is $3 + 6 = 9$; the sum of the digits in 72 is $7 + 2 = 9$. Adding the digits of a number to see whether they add up to nine can be a strategy in remembering a nines fact. For example, a student might think, "Let me see, does 9×6 equal 54 or 56? It must be 54 since $5 + 4$ is 9, but $5 + 6$ is not 9."

   3. The digit in the tens place in a nines fact is one less than the number being multiplied. For example, $4 \times 9 = 36$, and 3 is one less than 4. This can be combined with the previous pattern to derive nines facts. For example, 3×9 is in the twenties. Since $2 + 7$ is 9, 3×9 must be 27.

   4. Nines can easily be computed using the counting down strategy. Nine times a digit is the same as 10 times the digit, minus the digit. For example, 9×6 is $10 \times 6 - 6 = 54$.

B. Other patterns.

   Other patterns that are useful in remembering other special facts:

   1. 0 times a number equals 0.
   2. 1 times a number equals the number.
   3. 2 times a number is double the number.
   4. 5 times a number ends in 0 or 5; even numbers times 5 end in 0 and odd numbers times five end in 5.
   5. 10 times a number is the same number with a 0 on the end.

Sequencing the Study of Multiplication Facts

In kindergarten, children solve word problems involving multiplication situations. Beginning in first grade, the curriculum develops a conceptual foundation for multiplication through a variety of multiplication models, including repeated addition, the array model, and the number-line model. Fluency with the multiplication facts is expected by the end of third grade. Strategies are often introduced in specific, third-grade lessons. Practice is continued in subsequent lessons and especially in the Daily Practice and Problems and Home Practice. We do not introduce the multiplication facts in the order in which they are traditionally taught (first learning the 2s, then the

3s, then the 4s, etc.). Rather, we emphasize thinking strategies for the facts, introducing fact-groups in the following order:

2s, 3s, 5s, and 10s. The 2s, 3s, 5s, and 10s are easily solved using skip counting.

Square numbers such as $3 \times 3 = 9$, $4 \times 4 = 16$, and $5 \times 5 = 25$. These are introduced by arranging tiles into square arrays.

Nines. Students explore patterns for nines.

Last six facts. After students have learned the facts listed above and their turn-around facts ($9 \times 6 = 6 \times 9$), there are only six more facts to learn: 4×6, 4×7, 4×8, 6×7, 6×8, and 7×8.

Strategies for the Division Facts

The main strategy for learning the division facts is to think of the related multiplication fact. Therefore, students review the multiplication facts and develop fluency with the division facts by working with fact families. (Fact families are groups of related facts. An example of a fact family is $3 \times 4 = 12$, $4 \times 3 = 12$, $12 \div 3 = 4$, and $12 \div 4 = 3$.)

Using the Right Strategy

Different strategies appeal to different students. Students should not feel overburdened with the need to determine which is the "correct" strategy for a given fact. We do not intend to give them a new layer of things to learn. For example, when asked to explain a strategy for a fact, a student may say, "I've used it so much that now I just remember it." "Just remembering" is obviously an efficient strategy. The purpose of suggesting and discussing various strategies is to give students other, perhaps helpful, ways of learning the facts and to give them the confidence to think problems through when necessary. Students should have the opportunity to choose the strategies that work best for them or to invent their own.

The *Math Trailblazers* math facts program pervades most of the curriculum's components. Work with math facts are in different kinds of lessons. These are described in this section.

Math Facts Lessons

Figure 6: *Discussing fact strategies*

Everyday Work

As students work on problems in the labs and activities, encourage them to use and discuss various strategies for solving math facts problems. A number of important goals can best be reached through such discussions.

One goal is to legitimize all valid strategies, even those that may be less efficient. When students see their intuitive methods recognized and validated, they tend to perceive mathematical knowledge as continuous with everyday knowledge and common sense. We thus hope to avoid the unfortunate tendency of many students to separate their knowledge of mathematics from their knowledge of the real world.

By discussing strategies as they arise in context, students and teachers can explore how the strategies work and can verify that they are being used properly. Students should come to realize that a fact strategy that gives wrong answers is not very useful.

A second goal of our approach is to encourage students to communicate mathematical ideas. There are several reasons to stress communication: Students can learn from one another; communicating a method requires higher orders of thinking than simply applying that method; and skill at communicating is important in itself. We are social creatures. Mathematics and science are social endeavors in which communication is crucial.

A third goal of encouraging discussions of various methods is to give the teacher opportunities to learn about how students think. Knowing more about students' thinking helps the teacher ask better questions and plan more effective lessons.

Strategy Lessons

We feel that occasionally it is appropriate for lessons to focus on certain strategies that are developmentally appropriate for most students. Our plan is to begin with simple strategies that should be accessible to all students and to progress gradually to more complex forms of reasoning. For example, in the fall of first grade, we have several lessons that stress counting on to solve certain addition problems. Later, we explicitly introduce making a 10 and other, more sophisticated, strategies.

In general, you should expect your students to come up with effective strategies on their own. Our strategy lessons are intended to explore how and why various strategies work and also to codify and organize the strategies the students invent. They are not meant to dictate the only appropriate strategy for a given problem or to discourage students from using strategies they understand and like. They should be seen as opportunities to discuss strategies that may be appropriate for many students and to encourage their wider use.

Our ultimate goal is to produce students who can think mathematically, who can solve problems and deal easily with quantified information, and who enjoy mathematics and are not afraid of it. It is easier to do all of the above if one has fluency with the basic math facts. Practice strengthens students' abilities to use strategies and moves students towards fluency with the facts. Practice that follows instruction that stresses the use of strategies has been shown to improve students' fluency with the math facts. We recommend, and have incorporated into the curriculum, the following practice to gain this fluency.

Practice in Context

The primary practice of math facts will arise naturally for the students as they participate in the labs and other activities in the curriculum. These labs and activities offer many opportunities to practice addition, subtraction, multiplication, and division in a meaningful way. The lessons involve the student visually with drawings and patterns, auditorily through discussion, and tactilely through the use of many tools such as manipulatives and calculators.

Pages of problems on the basic facts are not only unnecessary, they can be counterproductive. Students may come to regard mathematics as mostly memorization and may perceive it as meaningless and unconnected to their everyday lives.

Structured Practice

Student-friendly, structured practice is built into the curriculum, especially in the DPP, Home Practice, and games. One small group of related math facts is presented to the students at a time. The practice of groups of facts is carefully distributed throughout the year. A small set of facts grouped in a meaningful way leads students to develop strategies such as adding doubles, counting back, or using a 10 for dealing with a particular situation. Furthermore, a small set of facts is a manageable amount to learn and remember.

Beginning in the second half of first grade and continuing through fifth grade, a small group of facts to be studied in a unit is introduced in the DPP. Through DPP items, students practice the facts and take a short assessment. Beginning in second grade, students use flash cards for additional practice with specific groups of facts. Facts are also practiced in many word problems in the DPP, Home Practice, and individual lessons. These problems allow students to focus on other interesting mathematical ideas as they also gain more fact practice.

Games

A variety of games are included in the curriculum, both in the lessons and in the DPP items of many units. A summary of the games used in a particular grade can be found in the Games section. Once students learn the rules of the games, they should play them periodically in class and at home for homework. Games provide an opportunity to encourage family involvement in the math program. When a game is assigned for homework, a note can be sent home with a place for the family members to sign, affirming that they played the game with their student.

Practice

Figure 7: *Playing a game*

Use of Calculators

The relationship between knowing the math facts and the use of calculators is an interesting one. Using a multiplication table or a calculator when necessary to find a fact helps promote familiarity and reinforces the math facts. Students soon figure out that it is quicker and more efficient to know the basic facts than to have to use these tools. The use of calculators also requires excellent estimation skills so that one can easily check for errors in calculator computations. Rather than eliminating the need for fluency with the facts, successful calculator use for solving complex problems depends on fact knowledge.

When to Practice

Practicing small groups of facts often for short periods of time is more effective than practicing many facts less often for long periods of time. For example, practicing 8 to 10 subtraction facts for 5 minutes several times a week is better than practicing all the subtraction facts for half an hour once a week. Good times for practicing the facts for 5 or 10 minutes during the school day include the beginning of the day, the beginning of math class, when students have completed an assignment, when an impending activity is delayed, or when an activity ends earlier than expected. Practicing small groups of facts at home involves parents in the process and frees class time for more interesting mathematics.

Practicing small groups of facts often for short periods of time is more effective than practicing many facts less often for long periods of time.

Assessment

Throughout the curriculum, teachers assess students' knowledge of the facts through observations as they work on activities, labs, and games. In Grades 3–5, students can use their *Facts I Know* charts to record their own progress in learning the facts. This type of self-assessment is very important in helping each student to become responsible for his or her own learning. Students are able to personalize their study of facts and not waste valuable time studying facts they already know.

In the second half of first grade, a sequence of facts assessments is provided in the Daily Practice and Problems. A more comprehensive facts assessment program begins in second grade. This program assesses students' progress in learning the facts, as outlined in the Expectations by Grade Level section of this tutor. As students develop strategies for a given group of facts, short quizzes accompany the practice. Students know which facts will be tested, focus practice in class and at home on those facts, then take the quiz. As they take the quiz, they use one color pencil to write answers before a given time limit, then use another color to complete the problems they need more time to answer. Students then use their *Facts I Know* charts to make a record of those facts they answered quickly, those facts they answered correctly but with less efficient strategies, and those facts they did not know at all. Using this information, students can concentrate their efforts on gaining fluency with those facts they answered correctly, but not quickly. They also know to develop strategies for those facts they could not answer at all. In this way, the number of facts studied at any one time becomes more manageable, practice becomes more meaningful, and the process less intimidating.

Tests of all the facts for any operation have a very limited role. They are used no more than two times a year to show growth over time and should not be given daily or weekly. Since we rarely, if ever, need to recall 100 facts at one time in everyday life, overemphasizing tests of all the facts reinforces the notion that math is nothing more than rote memorization and has no connection to the real world. Quizzes of small numbers of facts are as effective and not as threatening. They give students, parents, and teachers the information needed to continue learning and practicing efficiently. With an assessment approach based on strategies and the use of small groups of facts, students can see mathematics as connected to their own thinking and gain confidence in their mathematical abilities.

Conclusion

Research provides clear indications for curriculum developers and teachers about the design of effective math facts instruction. These recommendations formed the foundation of the *Math Trailblazers* math facts program. Developing strategies for learning the facts (rather than relying on rote memorization), distributing practice of small groups of facts, applying math facts in interesting problems, and using an appropriate assessment program—all are consistent with recommendations from current research. It is an instructional approach that encourages students to make sense of the mathematics they are learning. The resulting program will add efficiency and effectiveness to your students' learning of the math facts.

References

Ashlock, R.B., and C.A. Washbon. "Games: Practice Activities for the Basic Facts." In M.N. Suydam and R.E. Reys (eds.), *Developing Computational Skills: 1978 Yearbook.* National Council of Teachers of Mathematics, Reston, VA, 1978.

Beattie, L.D. "Children's Strategies for Solving Subtraction-Fact Combinations." *Arithmetic Teacher,* 27 (1), pp. 14–15, 1979.

Brownell, W.A., and C.B. Chazal. "The Effects of Premature Drill in Third-Grade Arithmetic." *Journal of Educational Research,* 29 (1), 1935.

Carpenter, T.P., and J.M. Moser. "The Acquisition of Addition and Subtraction Concepts in Grades One through Three." *Journal for Research in Mathematics Education,* 15 (3), pp. 179–202, 1984.

Cook, C.J., and J.A. Dossey. "Basic Fact Thinking Strategies for Multiplication—Revisited." *Journal for Research in Mathematics Education,* 13 (3), pp. 163–171, 1982.

Davis, E.J. "Suggestions for Teaching the Basic Facts of Arithmetic." In M.N. Suydam and R.E. Reys (eds.), *Developing Computational Skills: 1978 Yearbook.* National Council of Teachers of Mathematics, Reston, VA, 1978.

Fuson, K.C. "Teaching Addition, Subtraction, and Place-Value Concepts." In L. Wirszup and R. Streit (eds.), *Proceedings of the UCSMP International Conference on Mathematics Education: Developments in School Mathematics Education Around the World: Applications-Oriented Curricula and Technology-Supported Learning for All Students.* National Council of Teachers of Mathematics, Reston, VA, 1987.

Fuson, K.C., and G.B. Willis. "Subtracting by Counting Up: More Evidence." *Journal for Research in Mathematics Education,* 19 (5), pp. 402–420, 1988.

Fuson, K.C., J.W. Stigler, and K. Bartsch. "Grade Placement of Addition and Subtraction Topics in Japan, Mainland China, the Soviet Union, Taiwan, and the United States." *Journal for Research in Mathematics Education,* 19 (5), pp. 449–456, 1988.

Greer, B. "Multiplication and Division as Models of Situations." In D.A. Grouws (ed.), *Handbook of Research on Mathematics Teaching and Learning: A Project of the National Council of Teachers of Mathematics* (Chapter 13). Macmillan, New York, 1992.

Hiebert, James. "Relationships between Research and the NCTM Standards." *Journal for Research in Mathematics Education,* 30 January, pp. 3–19, 1999.

Isaacs, A.C., and W.M. Carroll. "Strategies for Basic Facts Instruction." *Teaching Children Mathematics,* 5 May, pp. 508–515, 1999.

Kouba, V.L., C.A. Brown, T.P. Carpenter, M.M. Lindquist, E.A. Silver, and J.O. Swafford. "Results of the Fourth NAEP Assessment of Mathematics: Number, Operations, and Word Problems." *Arithmetic Teacher,* 35 (8), pp. 14–19, 1988.

Myers, A.C., and C.A. Thornton. "The Learning-Disabled Child—Learning the Basic Facts." *Arithmetic Teacher,* 25 (3), pp. 46–50, 1977.

National Research Council. *Adding It Up: Helping Children Learn Mathematics.* National Academy Press, Washington, DC, 2001.

Principles and Standards for School Mathematics. National Council of Teachers of Mathematics, Reston, VA, 2000.

Rathmell, E.C. "Using Thinking Strategies to Teach the Basic Facts." In M.N. Suydam and R.E. Reys (eds.), *Developing Computational Skills: 1978 Yearbook.* National Council of Teachers of Mathematics, Reston, VA, 1978.

Rathmell, E.C., and P.R. Trafton. "Whole Number Computation." In J.N. Payne (ed.), *Mathematics for the Young Child.* National Council of Teachers of Mathematics, Reston, VA, 1990.

Swart, W.L. "Some Findings on Conceptual Development of Computational Skills." *Arithmetic Teacher,* 32 (5), pp. 36–38, 1985.

Thornton, C.A. "Doubles Up—Easy!" *Arithmetic Teacher,* 29 (8), p. 20, 1982.

Thornton, C.A. "Emphasizing Thinking Strategies in Basic Fact Instruction." *Journal for Research in Mathematics Education,* 9 (3), pp. 214–227, 1978.

Thornton, C.A. "Solution Strategies: Subtraction Number Facts." *Educational Studies in Mathematics,* 21 (1), pp. 241–263, 1990.

Thornton, C.A. "Strategies for the Basic Facts." In J.N. Payne (ed.), *Mathematics for the Young Child.* National Council of Teachers of Mathematics, Reston, VA, 1990.

Thornton, C.A., and P.J. Smith. "Action Research: Strategies for Learning Subtraction Facts." *Arithmetic Teacher,* 35 (8), pp. 8–12, 1988.

Van de Walle, J. *Elementary and Middle School Mathematics: Teaching Developmentally.* Addison Wesley, New York, 2001.

Math Facts Calendar
Grade 5

The Grade 5 Math Facts Calendar outlines an alternative distribution of math facts practice, assessment, and review. The alternative schedule is intended for use in classrooms that are moving significantly slower through the units than is recommended in the Unit Outlines in the *Unit Resource Guides* and in the Overview section of the *Teacher Implementation Guide.* For those classrooms, following the alternative schedule will ensure that students receive a comprehensive math facts program.

All of the materials referenced in the Math Facts Calendar are located elsewhere in *Math Trailblazers* as well as the *Grade 5 Facts Resource Guide.*

The elements included in the Math Facts Calendar are described below.

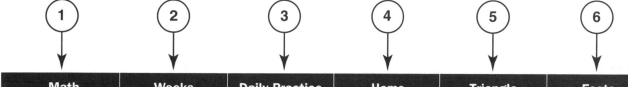

Math Facts Groups	Weeks	Daily Practice and Problems	Home Practice	Triangle Flash Cards	Facts Quizzes and Tests
Multiplication and Division: 2s and 3s	6–8	Unit 3: items 3B, 3C, 3D, 3E, 3I, 3K, 3O & 3U	Unit 3 Part 1	*Triangle Flash Cards: 2s and 3s*	DPP item 3U is a quiz on the 2s and 3s. The *Multiplication and Division Facts I Know* charts are updated.
Multiplication and Division: Square Numbers	9–12	Unit 4: items 4B, 4E, 4I, 4K, 4M, 4S, 4Z & 4AA	Unit 4 Part 1	*Triangle Flash Cards: Square Numbers*	DPP item 4AA is a quiz on the square numbers. The *Multiplication and Division Facts I Know* charts are updated.
Multiplication and Division: 9s	13–15	Unit 5: items 5B, 5C, 5D, 5E, 5I, 5K, 5O & 5S	Unit 5 Part 1	*Triangle Flash Cards: 9s*	DPP item 5S is a quiz on the 9s. The *Multiplication* and *Division Facts I Know* charts are updated.

Math Facts Groups

The *Math Trailblazers* program for reviewing the multiplication and division facts is organized into five groups of facts. This column describes which math facts are to be reviewed, practiced, and assessed.

Weeks

The *Math Trailblazers* math facts program is integrated into each unit. Formal practice and assessment of the math facts are distributed throughout the school year, largely in the Daily Practice and Problems (DPP). The fifth-grade math facts program focuses on review and assessment of the multiplication and division facts. Classrooms that roughly follow the schedule indicated in the Unit Outlines will not need to consider an alternative schedule for math fact practice—work in the units includes a comprehensive program for reviewing and assessing the multiplication and division facts.

Week 1 in the alternative schedule refers to the first week of school. Week 2 refers to the second week of school, and so on.

Daily Practice and Problems

The DPP items from each unit that focus on the math facts are listed in this column.

The Daily Practice and Problems (DPP) is a series of short exercises designed to:

- provide distributed practice in computation and a structure for systematic review of the basic math facts;
- develop concepts and skills such as number sense, mental math, telling time, and working with money throughout the year; and
- review topics, presenting concepts in new contexts and linking ideas from unit to unit.

There are three types of items: Bits, Tasks, and Challenges. Most are written so that they can be quickly copied onto the blackboard.

- Bits are short and should take no more than five or ten minutes to complete. They often provide practice with a skill or the basic math facts.
- Tasks take ten to fifteen minutes to complete.
- Challenges usually take longer than fifteen minutes to complete and the problems are more thought provoking. They stretch students' problem-solving skills.

The DPP may be used in class for practice and review, as assessment, or for homework. Notes for teachers provide answers as well as suggestions for using the items. Only those DPP items that focus on the math facts are listed here.

For more information on the Daily Practice and Problems, see the Daily Practice and Problems and Home Practice Guide in the *Teacher Implementation Guide*.

Home Practice

The Home Practice is a series of problems, located in the *Discovery Assignment Book,* that are designed to be sent home with students to supplement homework assignments. Each Home Practice is divided into several parts that can be assigned separately. Part 1 of the Home Practice in Units 3–8 recommends use of *Triangle Flash Cards* for practice of specific groups of facts. As part of the Home Practice assignments, students also update their *Facts I Know* charts.

For more information on the Home Practice, see the Daily Practice and Problems and Home Practice Guide in the *Teacher Implementation Guide.*

Triangle Flash Cards

As part of the DPP and Home Practice in Units 2–8 of fifth grade, students use the *Triangle Flash Cards* to practice and assess their knowledge of specific groups of math facts. Students categorize facts into three groups (facts I know quickly, facts I know using a strategy, and facts I need to learn). They record this information on a chart that is updated regularly.

The *Triangle Flash Cards* are distributed in Units 2–6 in the *Discovery Assignment Book.* Copies of the *Triangle Flash Cards* are also included in Section 7 of the *Grade 5 Facts Resource Guide.* The *Multiplication* and *Division Facts I Know* charts are distributed as part of the *Facts I Know* lesson (Unit 2 Lesson 2), which is reproduced in Section 5 of the *Grade 5 Facts Resource Guide.*

Facts Quizzes and Tests

Periodic quizzes of small groups of math facts are given as part of the DPP. Facts are grouped to encourage the use of strategies in learning facts. In fifth grade, an inventory test of the multiplication and division facts in all the groups is given in Unit 8.

Grade 5 Math Facts Calendar

Math Facts Groups	Weeks	Daily Practice and Problems	Home Practice	Triangle Flash Cards	Facts Quizzes and Tests
Addition and Subtraction Review	1–2	Unit 1: items 1B, 1C, 1E, 1K & 1O	Unit 1 Part 1		DPP items 1C and 1E can serve as addition fact inventory tests. DPP Items 1K and 1O can serve as subtraction fact inventory tests.
Multiplication and Division: 5s and 10s	3–5	The lesson *Facts I Know* (Unit 2 Lesson 2) begins the formal Grade 5 math facts review. Complete that lesson prior to beginning the DPP items listed below. Unit 2: items 2I, 2M, 2O, 2Q, 2U, 2W, 2X, 2Y, 2AA & 2CC	Unit 2 Part 1	*Triangle Flash Cards: 5s and 10s*	DPP item 2CC is a quiz on the 5s and 10s. The *Multiplication and Division Facts I Know* charts are updated.
Multiplication and Division: 2s and 3s	6–8	Unit 3: items 3B, 3C, 3D, 3E, 3I, 3K, 3O & 3U	Unit 3 Part 1	*Triangle Flash Cards: 2s and 3s*	DPP item 3U is a quiz on the 2s and 3s. The *Multiplication and Division Facts I Know* charts are updated.
Multiplication and Division: Square Numbers	9–12	Unit 4: items 4B, 4E, 4I, 4K, 4M, 4S, 4Z & 4AA	Unit 4 Part 1	*Triangle Flash Cards: Square Numbers*	DPP item 4AA is a quiz on the square numbers. The *Multiplication and Division Facts I Know* charts are updated.
Multiplication and Division: 9s	13–15	Unit 5: items 5B, 5C, 5D, 5E, 5I, 5K, 5O & 5S	Unit 5 Part 1	*Triangle Flash Cards: 9s*	DPP item 5S is a quiz on the 9s. The *Multiplication and Division Facts I Know* charts are updated.
Multiplication and Division: The Last Six Facts	16–18	Unit 6: items 6B, 6D, 6E, 6G, 6K, 6O, 6P & 6Q	Unit 6 Part 1	*Triangle Flash Cards: Last Six Facts*	DPP item 6Q is a quiz on the last six facts. The *Multiplication and Division Facts I Know* charts are updated.
Multiplication and Division: Review All Fact Groups	19–25	Unit 7: items 7C, 7G, 7K, 7O, 7S & 7W Unit 8: items 8B, 8C, 8I, 8K, 8M & 8Q	Unit 7 Part 1 Unit 8 Part 1	*Triangle Flash Cards: 5s, 10s, 2s, 3s, Square Numbers, 9s, and the Last Six Facts*	DPP item 8Q is an inventory test on all five groups of multiplication and division facts. The *Multiplication and Division Facts I Know* charts are updated.

Grade 5 Math Facts Calendar *(continued)*

Math Facts Groups	Weeks	Daily Practice and Problems	Home Practice	Triangle Flash Cards	Facts Quizzes and Tests
Multiplication and Division: Review (without formal assessment) **Distribute these items over the remainder of the school year.**	26–39	Unit 9: items 9G, 9K, 9M, 9Q & 9S Unit 10: items 10A, 10E, 10I, 10K & 10O Unit 11: items 11E, 11I, 11M, 11P, 11Q, 11S & 11U Unit 12: items 12A, 12E, 12G, 12I, 12K & 12M Unit 13: items 13A, 13E, 13H, 13I, 13M, 13Q & 13S Unit 14: items 14E, 14G, 14K, 14O, 14P, 14S & 14W Unit 15: items 15E, 15F & 15I Unit 16: items 16E, 16G, 16I, 16O & 16S	Unit 12 Part 2 Unit 13 Part 1 Unit 15 Parts 1 & 2		

Section 5

Facts Distribution
Addition and Subtraction:
Review • Weeks 1–2

Math Facts Groups	Weeks	Daily Practice and Problems	Home Practice	Triangle Flash Cards	Facts Quizzes and Tests
Addition and Subtraction Review	1–2	Unit 1: items 1B, 1C, 1E, 1K & 1O	Unit 1 Part 1		DPP items 1C and 1E can serve as addition fact inventory tests. DPP items 1K and 1O can serve as subtraction fact inventory tests.

Daily Practice and Problems

Students may solve the items individually, in groups, or as a class. The items may also be assigned for homework. The DPPs are also available on the Teacher Resource CD.

Student Questions	Teacher Notes

1B Who Am I?

I am greater than 5 + 6 but less than 12 + 8.

I am an even number.

If you skip count by 3s, you'll say me.

I am not 18.

Write a riddle of your own. Exchange it with a friend.

TIMS Task

12

1C Addition Review 1

Solve the following using paper and pencil only.

A.　64
　+81

B.　43
　+94

C.　85
　+82

D.　92
　+57

E.　81
　+93

F.　60
　+96

G.　74
　+85

H.　92
　+92

I.　46
　+73

J.　50
　+58

K.　32
　+82

L.　69
　+60

TIMS Bit

Since these addition problems do not involve any regrouping, they can be used to assess students' fluency with the addition facts. These problems, along with those in DPP item 1E, include most of the basic addition facts students should know. If some students need addition fact practice, assign them activities, games, and flash cards from the *Addition and Subtraction Math Facts Review* in Section 8.

A. 145　　B. 137
C. 167　　D. 149
E. 174　　F. 156
G. 159　　H. 184
I. 119　　J. 108
K. 114　　L. 129

Addition Review 2

TIMS Bit

Solve the following using paper and pencil only.

A.	75 +33	B.	72 +94	C.	54 +84

Like the problems in DPP item 1C, these addition problems do not involve any regrouping. Thus they can be used to assess students' fluency with the addition facts. These problems, along with those in DPP item 1C, include most of the basic addition facts students should know. If some students need addition fact practice, assign them activities, games, and flash cards from the *Addition and Subtraction Math Facts Review* in Section 8.

D.	53 +72	E.	88 +21	F.	63 +73

A. 108	B. 166
C. 138	D. 125
E. 109	F. 136
G. 128	H. 110
I. 117	J. 122
K. 108	L. 147

G.	46 +82	H.	50 +60	I.	27 +90

J.	31 +91	K.	47 +61	L.	71 +76

1K **Subtraction Review 1**

Solve the following using paper and pencil only.

A.	1462	B.	1030	C.	1176
	− 750		− 810		− 842

D.	1096	E.	1067	F.	1192
	− 435		− 532		− 962

G.	1255	H.	1685	I.	1234
	− 741		− 941		− 632

J.	1715	K.	1483	L.	1597
	− 902		− 851		− 975

TIMS Bit

Use this item and item 1O as inventory tests for subtraction fact recall. No regrouping is involved in any of the problems. If some students need practice with the subtraction facts, assign them activities, games, and flash cards from the *Addition and Subtraction Math Facts Review* in Section 8.

A.	712	B.	220
C.	334	D.	661
E.	535	F.	230
G.	514	H.	744
I.	602	J.	813
K.	632	L.	622

1O **Subtraction Review 2**

Solve the following using paper and pencil.

A.	1079	B.	1353	C.	1669
	− 772		− 852		− 845

D.	1397	E.	1265	F.	1478
	− 901		− 963		− 936

G.	1887	H.	1291	I.	1198
	− 926		− 881		− 943

J.	1548	K.	1379	L.	1184
	− 837		− 657		− 784

TIMS Bit

Use this item and item 1K as inventory tests for subtraction fact recall. No regrouping is involved in any of the problems. If some students need practice, assign them activities, games, and flash cards from the *Addition and Subtraction Math Facts Review* in Section 8.

A.	307	B.	501
C.	824	D.	496
E.	302	F.	542
G.	961	H.	410
I.	255	J.	711
K.	722	L.	400

Unit 1 Home Practice

PART 1 Addition and Subtraction

Solve the following problems in your head.

A. 30 + 90 = _____

B. 50 + 60 = _____

C. 160 − 90 = _____

D. 148 − 50 = _____

E. 240 + 80 = _____

F. 100 − 32 = _____

G. 650 + 250 = _____

H. 732 + 632 = _____

I. 389 + 11 = _____

On another sheet of paper, explain how you solved two of the problems in your head.

 **Section 5**

Facts Distribution
Multiplication and Division: 5s and 10s • Weeks 3–5

Math Facts Groups	Weeks	Daily Practice and Problems	Home Practice	Triangle Flash Cards	Facts Quizzes and Tests
Multiplication and Division: 5s and 10s	3–5	The lesson *Facts I Know* (Unit 2 Lesson 2) begins the formal Grade 5 math facts review. Complete that lesson prior to beginning the DPP items listed below. Unit 2: items 2I, 2M, 2O, 2Q, 2U, 2W, 2X, 2Y, 2AA & 2CC	Unit 2 Part 1	*Triangle Flash Cards: 5s and 10s*	DPP item 2CC is a quiz on the 5s and 10s. The *Multiplication* and *Division Facts I Know* charts are updated.

Daily Practice and Problems

Students may solve the items individually, in groups, or as a class. The items may also be assigned for homework. The DPPs are also available on the Teacher Resource CD.

Student Questions	Teacher Notes

 Multiplication and Division Sentences

Lin has 15 flowers to place in 3 vases. How many flowers go in each vase if she divides them evenly?

A. Draw a picture to illustrate this problem.

B. Write a multiplication sentence and a division sentence that describe this problem.

TIMS Bit

A. Pictures will vary, but the important idea here is that division can be used to arrange a group of objects into smaller, equal-sized groups.

B. 3 vases × 5 flowers in each vase = 15 flowers;
15 flowers ÷ 3 vases = 5 flowers in each vase

 More Multiplication and Division Sentences

There are 20 students in gym class. They divide into pairs to practice sit-ups. How many pairs of students will practice sit-ups?

A. Draw a picture to illustrate this problem.

B. Write a multiplication sentence and a division sentence to describe this problem.

TIMS Task

A. Pictures will vary.

B. 2 students per pair ×
10 pairs = 20 students;
20 students ÷ 2 students per pair = 10 pairs

 A Juicy Problem

Two shipments of fruit were delivered to the school cafeteria. One shipment contained 8 sacks of oranges, 50 pounds to a sack. In the other shipment, there were 7 sacks, also 50 pounds to a sack. How many pounds of fruit were delivered to the cafeteria in all?

TIMS Bit

First shipment = 400 pounds

Second shipment = 350 pounds

750 pounds of fruit were delivered in all.

or

15 sacks × 50 pounds per sack = 750 pounds

Student Questions	Teacher Notes

2Q Facts for 5s and 10s

A. $10 \times 3 =$

B. $35 \div 5 =$

C. $80 \div 10 =$

D. $9 \times 5 =$

E. $5 \times 10 =$

F. $25 \div 5 =$

G. $10 \times 10 =$

TIMS Bit

A. 30   B. 7

C. 8   D. 45

E. 50   F. 5

G. 100

2U Patterns with Zeros

Do these problems in your head.

A. $5 \times 3 =$

B. $5 \times 30 =$

C. $5 \times 300 =$

D. $5 \times 3000 =$

E. $5 \times 30,000 =$

What is the pattern when you multiply numbers that end in zero?

TIMS Bit

A. 15

B. 150

C. 1500

D. 15,000

E. 150,000

Students should see that in these problems the number of zeros in each product is equal to the number of zeros in the problem.

2W Multiplying by Numbers Ending in Zeros

A. $50 \times 7 =$

B. $600 \times 50 =$

C. $60 \times 10 =$

D. $800 \times 100 =$

E. $500 \times 9 =$

F. $200 \times 5000 =$

TIMS Bit

A. 350

B. 30,000

C. 600

D. 80,000

E. 4500

F. 1,000,000

2X **Related Facts**

Solve each problem. Then name a related division sentence for each.

A. $500 \times 5 = ?$

B. $10 \times 30 = ?$

C. $1000 \times 5 = ?$

D. $400 \times 50 = ?$

TIMS Task

A. 2500; $2500 \div 5 = 500$ or $2500 \div 500 = 5$

B. 300; $300 \div 10 = 30$ or $300 \div 30 = 10$

C. 5000; $5000 \div 5 = 1000$ or $5000 \div 1000 = 5$

D. 20,000; $20,000 \div 50 = 400$ or $20,000 \div 400 = 50$

2Y **More Multiplication with Numbers Ending in Zero**

Find the missing number, *n*, in each sentence to make that sentence true.

A. $100 \times n = 5000$

B. $50 \times n = 25,000$

C. $500 \times n = 35,000$

D. $n \times 100 = 10,000$

E. $500 \times 40 = n$

F. $n \times 80 = 4000$

TIMS Bit

A. 50

B. 500

C. 70

D. 100

E. 20,000

F. 50

2AA **Facts for 5s and 10s**

A. $5 \times 6 =$ B. $10 \times 9 =$

C. $40 \div 5 =$ D. $40 \div 10 =$

E. $6 \times 10 =$ F. $10 \div 2 =$

G. $70 \div 7 =$ H. $4 \times 5 =$

TIMS Bit

A. 30   B. 90

C. 8   D. 4

E. 60   F. 5

G. 10   H. 20

Quiz: 5s and 10s

A. $7 \times 5 =$　　　　B. $40 \div 4 =$

C. $10 \div 2 =$　　　D. $8 \times 10 =$

E. $9 \times 5 =$　　　　F. $6 \times 10 =$

G. $30 \div 6 =$　　　H. $10 \times 2 =$

I. $15 \div 5 =$　　　　J. $70 \div 10 =$

K. $40 \div 8 =$　　　L. $5 \times 10 =$

M. $10 \times 3 =$　　　N. $25 \div 5 =$

O. $90 \div 9 =$　　　P. $4 \times 5 =$

Q. $10 \times 10 =$

TIMS Bit

We recommend 5 minutes for this quiz. You might want to allow students to change pens after the time is up and complete the remaining problems in a different color. After students take the test, have them update their *Multiplication Facts I Know* and *Division Facts I Know* charts.

Unit 2 Home Practice

PART 1 *Triangle Flash Cards: 5s and 10s*

Study for the quiz on the multiplication and division facts for the 5s and 10s. Take home your *Triangle Flash Cards: 5s* and *10s* and your list of facts you need to study.

Ask a family member to choose one flash card at a time. To quiz you on a multiplication fact, he or she should cover the corner containing the highest number. (The highest number on each card is lightly shaded.) This number will be the answer to two multiplication facts. Multiply the two uncovered numbers.

$5 \times 4 = ?$

$4 \times 5 = ?$

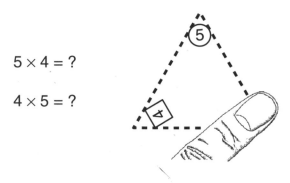

To quiz you on a division fact, your family member can cover the number in the square. Then you use the two uncovered numbers to solve a division fact. Your family member can then cover the number inside the circle to quiz you on a related division fact.

$20 \div 5 = ?$ $20 \div 4 = ?$

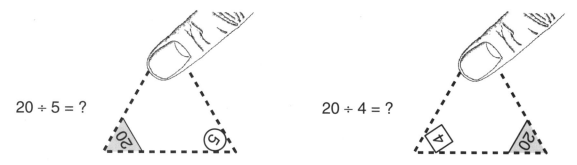

Ask your family member to mix up the multiplication and division facts. He or she should sometimes cover the highest number, sometimes cover the circled number, and sometimes cover the number in the square.

Your teacher will tell you when the quiz on the 5s and 10s will be given.

Lesson 2

Facts I Know

Lesson Overview

Estimated Class Sessions

1-2

This lesson introduces the yearlong review of the multiplication and division facts. Students use flash cards to review the multiplication and division facts for the first group of facts, the 5s and 10s. They record on charts both the multiplication and division facts they know and can answer quickly. They will continue to update these charts throughout the year. Specific DPP items in Unit 2 continue the practice of the 5s and 10s. In the DPP for Units 3–6 the other four groups of facts (2s and 3s, squares, 9s, and the last six facts—4 × 6, 4 × 7, 4 × 8, 6 × 7, 6 × 8, and 7 × 8) are practiced and assessed.

Key Content

- Self-assessing the multiplication and division facts.
- Maintaining fluency with the multiplication and division facts.

Key Vocabulary

- divisor
- fact families
- factors
- product
- quotient
- turn-around facts

Homework

Assign Part 1 of the Home Practice that asks students to practice the math facts.

Assessment

1. Students use flash cards and *Facts I Know* charts to assess themselves on the multiplication and division facts.
2. Record your observations on the *Observational Assessment Record.*

Curriculum Sequence

Multiplication and Division Facts

Students using *Math Trailblazers* are expected to demonstrate fluency with the multiplication facts by the end of third grade. By the end of fourth grade, they are expected to demonstrate fluency with the division facts.

Students develop conceptual understanding and procedures for multiplication in third grade. The introduction of strategies to gain fluency with the multiplication facts begins in Unit 11 of third grade. A systematic approach to gaining fluency with the division facts is a component of the fourth-grade curriculum.

Multiplication and Division Facts

By the end of fourth grade, students in *Math Trailblazers* are expected to demonstrate fluency with all the facts. This lesson, which focuses on the 5s and 10s, begins a systematic review of the multiplication and division facts that will continue throughout the DPP in fifth grade. As students review each of five groups of multiplication facts, they study the related division facts. Using this approach, students maintain their fluency with the multiplication and division facts. The table below lists the five groups of facts and indicates when each is introduced in the DPP.

For a detailed explanation of our approach to learning and assessing the facts, see the *Grade 5 Facts Resource Guide.* Information is also in the TIMS Tutor: *Math Facts* in the *Teacher Implementation Guide* and *Information for Parents: Grade 5 Math Facts Philosophy,* which immediately follows the Unit 2 Background.

Unit	Math Fact Group
2	Group 1: 5s and 10s
3	Group 2: 2s and 3s
4	Group 3: squares
5	Group 4: 9s
6	Group 5: The last six facts: 4×6, 4×7, 4×8, 6×7, 6×8, 7×8
7	Review all five groups.
8	Assess all five groups.

Materials List

Supplies and Copies

Student	Teacher
Supplies for Each Student • ruler • scissors	**Supplies** • scissors
Copies • 1 copy of *Multiplication* and *Division Facts I Know* charts per student (*Unit Resource Guide* Pages 61–62) • 1 copy of *Information for Parents: Grade 5 Math Facts Philosophy* per student (*Unit Resource Guide* Pages 13–14) • 1 copy of *Centimeter Dot Paper* per student (*Unit Resource Guide* Page 63)	**Copies/Transparencies** • 1 transparency of *Triangle Flash Cards: 5s* (*Discovery Assignment Book* Page 21) • 1 transparency of *Triangle Flash Cards: 10s* (*Discovery Assignment Book* Page 23) • 1 transparency of *Centimeter Dot Paper* (*Unit Resource Guide* Page 63) • 1 copy of *Observational Assessment Record* to be used throughout this unit (*Unit Resource Guide* Pages 15–16)

All blackline masters including assessment, transparency, and DPP masters are also on the Teacher Resource CD.

Student Books

Facts I Know (*Student Guide* Pages 35–38)
Triangle Flash Cards: 5s (*Discovery Assignment Book* Page 21)
Triangle Flash Cards: 10s (*Discovery Assignment Book* Page 23)

Daily Practice and Problems and Home Practice

DPP items E–F (*Unit Resource Guide* Page 21)
Home Practice Part 1 (*Discovery Assignment Book* Page 9)

Note: Classrooms whose pacing differs significantly from the suggested pacing of the units should use the Math Facts Calendar in Section 4 of the *Facts Resource Guide* to ensure students receive the complete math facts program.

Assessment Tools

Observational Assessment Record (*Unit Resource Guide* Pages 15–16)

Daily Practice and Problems

Suggestions for using the DPPs are on page 58.

E. Bit: Making Change (URG p. 21)

David buys a CD that costs $14.49 with tax. He gives the sales clerk a $20 bill. How much change will he receive? Name the least number of coins and bills he can receive.

F. Task: Measuring Pencils
(URG p. 21)

Measure the length of four classmates' pencils to the nearest centimeter. Record the information in a data table. Then find the median length of the pencils.

TIMS Tip

Although students work in pairs, each student needs a set of flash cards so he or she can sort the cards in class and at home. Students need the flash cards repeatedly throughout the Daily Practice and Problems and the Home Practice. Have students write their initials on the back of each card and save them in envelopes or folders for future use. Some teachers have students make two sets—one for home and one for school. Others laminate the cards for durability. Blackline masters of the cards are provided in the *Facts Resource Guide*. Use these masters throughout the year to make additional copies as the need arises.

Before the Activity

Each student needs *Triangle Flash Cards: 5s* and *10s* from the *Discovery Assignment Book* and one copy each of the *Multiplication Facts I Know* and *Division Facts I Know* charts. Send home a copy of the *Information for Parents: Grade 5 Math Facts Philosophy* with each student.

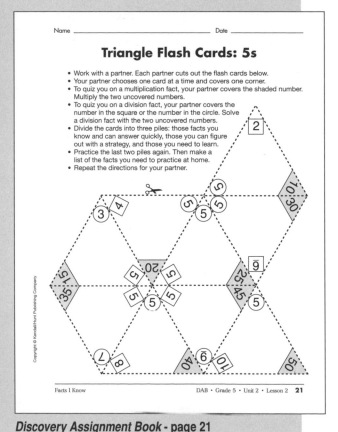

Discovery Assignment Book - page 21

Discovery Assignment Book - page 23

Part 1 Multiplication Facts and Triangle Flash Cards

The Multiplication Facts and Triangle Flash Cards section of the *Facts I Know* Activity Pages in the *Student Guide* introduces students to the use of Triangle Flash Cards. In this lesson students use *Triangle Flash Cards: 5s* and *10s* which are in the *Discovery Assignment Book.* Students who had *Math Trailblazers* in fourth grade will probably recognize the flash cards and remember how to use them. Read the directions in **Questions 1A and 1B** on the *Facts I Know* Activity Pages along with your students. To use the flash cards, one partner covers the corner containing the highest number with his or her thumb (this number is lightly shaded). This number is the answer—or **product**—to a multiplication problem. The second person multiplies the two uncovered numbers. These are the two **factors.** Partners should take turns quizzing each other on the multiplication facts for the 5s and 10s. As students are quizzed, they place each flash card into one of three piles: those facts they know and can answer quickly, those they can figure out with a strategy, and those they need to learn.

Once students sort all their cards, they record their results on their copies of the *Multiplication Facts I Know* chart, which is in the *Unit Resource Guide* **(Question 1C).** Figure 6 illustrates how to do this with one set of facts. Throughout the year, students will be reminded to update these charts.

TIMS Tip

To help students organize the three stacks of flash cards, they can cut an index card into three pieces. Then they write "Know Quickly" on one piece, "Know with Strategy" on another, and "Don't Know" on a third.

Content Note

Multiplication Facts. Since third grade, students in *Math Trailblazers* have used the term **turn-around facts** to describe multiplication facts that contain the same factors but in a different order. For example, $4 \times 5 = 20$ and $5 \times 4 = 20$ are turn-around facts.

When students begin their *Multiplication Facts I Know* charts, you might want to discuss the facts for 0s and 1s. Many students know these facts and will want to circle them right away. Have students explain multiplication by 0 and 1. Any number times 0 is 0. Any number times 1 is itself.

Facts I Know

Multiplication Facts and Triangle Flash Cards

1. Work with a partner. Use the directions below and your *Triangle Flash Cards: 5s* and *10s* to practice the multiplication facts.

   A. One partner covers the corner containing the highest number. (This number is lightly shaded on each triangle.) This number is the answer to a multiplication problem, called the **product.** The second person multiplies the two uncovered numbers which are called the **factors.**

   $5 \times 4 = ?$
   $4 \times 5 = ?$

   B. Place each flash card in one of three piles: those facts you know and can answer quickly, those you can figure out with a strategy, and those you need to learn.

   C. Begin your *Multiplication Facts I Know* chart. Circle those facts you know well and can answer quickly.

   For example, Felicia looked through the pile of facts she knew well and answered quickly. Felicia knew that $5 \times 4 = 20$ and $4 \times 5 = 20$. She circled two 20s on the chart. Look for the two other 20s on the chart. Why didn't Felicia circle these as well?

   Multiplication Facts I Know

×	0	1	2	3	4	5	6	7	8	9	10
0	0	0	0	0	0	0	0	0	0	0	0
1	0	1	2	3	4	5	6	7	8	9	10
2	0	2	4	6	8	10	12	14	16	18	20
3	0	3	6	9	12	15	18	21	24	27	30
4	0	4	8	12	16	⃝20	24	28	32	36	40
5	0	5	10	15	⃝20	25	30	35	40	45	50
6	0	6	12	18	24	30	36	42	48	54	60
7	0	7	14	21	28	35	42	49	56	63	70
8	0	8	16	24	32	40	48	56	64	72	80
9	0	9	18	27	36	45	54	63	72	81	90
10	0	10	20	30	40	50	60	70	80	90	100

   D. Discuss how you can figure out facts you don't recall right away. Share your strategies with your partner.

   E. Practice the last two piles at home for homework—the facts you can figure out with a strategy and those you need to learn. Make a list of those facts you need to practice.

Facts I Know   SG • Grade 5 • Unit 2 • Lesson 2   35

Student Guide - page 35 (Answers on p. 64)

Multiplication Facts I Know

×	0	1	2	3	4	5	6	7	8	9	10
0	0	0	0	0	0	0	0	0	0	0	0
1	0	1	2	3	4	5	6	7	8	9	10
2	0	2	4	6	8	10	12	14	16	18	20
3	0	3	6	9	12	15	18	21	24	27	30
4	0	4	8	12	16	⃝20	24	28	32	36	40
5	0	5	10	15	⃝20	25	30	35	40	45	50
6	0	6	12	18	24	30	36	42	48	54	60
7	0	7	14	21	28	35	42	49	56	63	70
8	0	8	16	24	32	40	48	56	64	72	80
9	0	9	18	27	36	45	54	63	72	81	90
10	0	10	20	30	40	50	60	70	80	90	100

Recording $4 \times 5 = 20$ and $5 \times 4 = 20$ as "Facts I Know."

Figure 6: *Circling a fact I know on the* Multiplication Facts I Know *chart*

Fact Families

2. The picture below models the following problem: *if a rectangle has a total of 20 squares organized in 4 rows, how many squares are in each row?*

What division sentence describes this problem?

3. The picture below models the following problem: *if a rectangle has a total of 20 squares organized in 5 rows, how many squares are in each row?*

What division sentence describes this problem?

4. What do you notice about the rectangles in Questions 2 and 3? (If you need to, draw both of these rectangles on a piece of *Dot Paper*. Cut them out and lay one on top of the other.)

5. What two multiplication sentences describe the two rectangles in Questions 2 and 3?

The four facts: $4 \times 5 = 20$
$5 \times 4 = 20$
$20 \div 4 = 5$
and $20 \div 5 = 4$ are related facts. We say they are in the same **fact family.**

Student Guide - page 36 *(Answers on p. 64)*

TIMS Tip

Remind students that rows go across and columns go up and down.

Question 1D asks students to discuss strategies for figuring out answers to the multiplication facts they need to practice. Some examples of strategies follow. For more information about math fact strategies, see the TIMS Tutor: *Math Facts* in the *Teacher Implementation Guide.*

- Skip counting: This strategy is only efficient for a small number of facts. $2 \times 3 = \ldots 2, 4, 6$.

- Doubling: 7×4 may be solved by doubling the answer to 7×2; $7 \times 2 = 14$; $14 + 14 = 28$.

- Using known facts: Knowing 5×5 is 25 may help in solving 5×6; $5 \times 5 = 25$; $25 + 5 = 30$.

- Patterns in the 9s: The sum of the digits of the products is 9. For example, $9 \times 5 = $ **45.**
$4 + 5 = 9$.

Students should not spend time practicing the facts they already know. Therefore, after the flash cards are sorted and the *Multiplication Facts I Know* charts have been updated, **Question 1E** asks students to list the facts in the other two piles—those they can figure out using a strategy and those they need to learn. Students should take this list home along with their flash cards to study the facts. Part 1 of the Home Practice reminds students to take home this list and their flash cards.

Part 2 **Fact Families**

Distribute a copy of *Centimeter Dot Paper* to each student. Pose the following problem: *If a rectangle on the dot paper is made up of 30 squares and there are 5 rows of squares, how many squares are in each row?* Have students solve the problem by creating such a rectangle on *Centimeter Dot Paper.* The rectangle should be made up of 5 rows of 6 squares. See Figure 7.

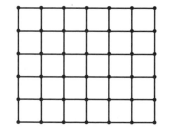

$5 \times ? = 30$

$30 \div 5 = ?$

Figure 7: *5 rows of 6 squares*

Ask students, *"What operation can you use to answer this question? Write a number sentence for the problem."* This question can be viewed as a multiplication problem with a missing number: $5 \times ? = 30$. It can also be viewed as a division problem: $30 \div 5 = ?$ Have students label their rectangles with both number sentences: $5 \times 6 = 30$ and $30 \div 5 = 6$.

Pose a similar problem: *If a rectangle is made up of 30 squares and there are 6 rows of squares, how many squares are in each row?* Ask students to solve this problem using the *Centimeter Dot Paper.* Your students should recognize that this problem results in a rectangle similar to the one they created earlier. This time there are 6 rows of 5 squares. Ask, *"What operation can you use to answer this question? Write a number sentence for the problem."* Both $6 \times ? = 30$ and $30 \div 6 = ?$ are appropriate number sentences. Ask students to label their second rectangle with both number sentences: $6 \times 5 = 30$ and $30 \div 6 = 5$. See Figure 8. Emphasize the fact that the two rectangles are the same, by having students cut out both rectangles and laying one directly on top of the other. You can demonstrate this using overhead transparencies of the *Centimeter Dot Paper.*

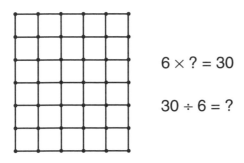

$6 \times ? = 30$

$30 \div 6 = ?$

Figure 8: *6 rows of 5 squares*

Since the four number sentences—$6 \times 5 = 30$, $5 \times 6 = 30$, $30 \div 5 = 6$, and $30 \div 6 = 5$—all represent the same rectangle, we can see that these four facts are related. Introduce students to the term fact family. These four related facts are in the same **fact family.**

If necessary, have students create more rectangles on *Centimeter Dot Paper* to illustrate fact families. *Questions 2–5* in the Fact Families section on the *Facts I Know* Activity Pages in the *Student Guide* provide another example using the facts 4×5, 5×4, $20 \div 4$, and $20 \div 5$. You may complete these questions as a class or have student pairs complete them. *Questions 6–11* provide multiplication and division fact practice for the 5s and 10s. Fact families are emphasized throughout. Students' knowledge of the multiplication facts and turn-around facts helps them review the division facts.

---

6. Solve each pair of related facts. Name two other facts in the same fact family.
   A. $5 \times 2 = ?$ and $2 \times 5 = ?$ **B.** $10 \times 3 = ?$ and $3 \times 10 = ?$
   C. $10 \times 5 = ?$ and $50 \div 10 = ?$ **D.** $6 \times 5 = ?$ and $30 \div 5 = ?$

7. Write the complete number sentence for each related fact.
   A. $8 \times 5 = $ _____   **B.** $7 \times 10 = $ _____
   _____ $\div 5 = $ _____   _____ $\div$ _____ $= 7$
   _____ $\div 8 = $ _____   _____ $\div 7 = $ _____
   $5 \times $ _____ $= $ _____ $10 \times $ _____ $= $ _____
   C. $90 \div $ _____ $= 9$ **D.** $5 \times $ _____ $= 45$
   _____ $\times 10 = $ _____ $45 \div $ _____ $= $ _____
   _____ $\div 9 = $ _____   _____ $\times 9 = $ _____
   _____ $\times 9 = $ _____ $45 \div $ _____ $= $ _____

8. What is 5×5? Name a related fact for 5×5. Is there more than one?

9. What is 10×10? Name a related fact for 10×10. Is there more than one?

10. The numbers 25 and 100 are square numbers. How are the fact families for the square numbers different from other fact families?

11. Solve the given fact. Then name other facts in the same fact family.
   A. $10 \times 6 = ?$ **B.** $20 \div 10 = ?$ **C.** $7 \times 5 = ?$ **D.** $80 \div 8 = ?$
   E. $15 \div 3 = ?$ **F.** $4 \times 10 = ?$ **G.** $3 \times 5 = ?$ **H.** $10 \div 2 = ?$

Division Facts and Triangle Flash Cards

12. With a partner, use the directions below and your *Triangle Flash Cards: 5s* and *10s* to practice the division facts.
   A. One partner covers the number in the square. This number will be the answer to a division problem, called the **quotient.** The number in the circle is the **divisor.** The second person solves a division fact with the two uncovered numbers as shown.

$20 \div 5 = ?$

Student Guide - page 37 (Answers on p. 65)

Student Guide - page 38 *(Answers on p. 65)*

Division Facts I Know

×	0	1	2	3	4	5	6	7	8	9	10
0	0	0	0	0	0	0	0	0	0	0	0
1	0	1	2	3	4	5	6	7	8	9	10
2	0	2	4	6	8	10	12	14	16	18	20
3	0	3	6	9	12	15	18	21	24	27	30
4	0	4	8	12	16	20	24	28	32	36	40
5	0	5	10	15	⑳	25	30	35	40	45	50
6	0	6	12	18	24	30	36	42	48	54	60
7	0	7	14	21	28	35	42	49	56	63	70
8	0	8	16	24	32	40	48	56	64	72	80
9	0	9	18	27	36	45	54	63	72	81	90
10	0	10	20	30	40	50	60	70	80	90	100

Divisor

Recording 20 ÷ 5 = 4 as a "Fact I Know."

Figure 10: *Using the* Division Facts I Know *chart*

Questions 8–10 focus on the square facts $5 \times 5 = 25$ and $10 \times 10 = 100$. Since the two factors in each of these number sentences are the same, the fact families for these are different from other families. $5 \times 5 = 25$ and $25 \div 5 = 5$ are the only two facts in this fact family. Likewise, $10 \times 10 = 100$ and $100 \div 10 = 10$ are the only two facts in this fact family.

Part 3 **Division Facts and Triangle Flash Cards**

After students practice the multiplication facts for the 5s and 10s by completing **Questions 6–11** in the *Student Guide,* have student pairs use their flash cards to assess the division facts. **Question 12** outlines how students can use the flash cards for division. The procedure here is similar to the way the cards were used earlier for multiplication. However, there is one difference. When using the cards for division, students need to sort the *Triangle Flash Cards: 5s* and *10s* twice. The first time through the cards, partners cover the numbers in squares **(Question 12A–12B).** Then, after sorting the cards, students update the *Division Facts I Know* chart **(Question 12C).** The second time through, partners cover the numbers in circles **(Question 12D).** After sorting the entire set of cards for the second time, students update their division chart **(Question 12E).** See Figure 9. Demonstrate this sequence using a transparency of the flash cards and the *Division Facts I Know* chart.

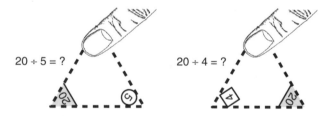

20 ÷ 5 = ?   20 ÷ 4 = ?

Figure 9: *Sort the cards twice—once covering the numbers in squares and a second time covering the numbers in circles.*

Question 12C provides an example of how to use the *Division Facts I Know* chart. Turn students' attention to the chart in **Question 12C.** Since Edward divided by 5 (20 ÷ 5 = 4), 5 is the **divisor.** He followed the 5 across its row to find the 20 he should circle. See Figure 10. Remind students that they circle only those facts that were in the pile of facts they know and can answer quickly. They should list the facts in the other two piles. Students should take this list home along with their flash cards to study the facts. Part 1 of the Home Practice reminds students to take home this list and their flash cards.

Question 13 asks students to compare their *Multiplication Facts I Know* chart with their *Division Facts I Know* chart. If students are using their knowledge of the multiplication facts and fact families to help them learn the division facts, they will see some patterns in their charts. For example, if a student knows 4×5 and 5×4, it is very likely he or she will know $20 \div 4$ and $20 \div 5$. Thus, two 20s should be circled on the division chart as well. Discuss students' results. Note that both *Facts I Know* charts have a multiplication symbol in the first square since both charts are simply multiplication tables used for recording known facts.

DPP items I, M, O, Q, U, W, X, Y, and AA, provide further practice with the multiplication and division facts for the 5s and 10s. A quiz on the 5s and 10s is provided in Item CC. Inform students when you will give the quiz so they can practice at home.

Part 4 Fact Practice in the DPP

Students practice the multiplication and division facts as they use them to solve problems in labs, activities, and games. However, the systematic practice and assessment of the math facts takes place primarily in the DPP. The study of math facts in the DPP for Units 3–6 parallels what takes place in Unit 2:

1. A DPP item instructs students to quiz each other on a group of facts using the *Triangle Flash Cards*. Students sort the cards into three piles as previously described. They update their *Multiplication* and *Division Facts I Know* charts.

2. Additional DPP items provide practice with the multiplication and division fact families for a particular group.

3. A final DPP item includes a quiz that assesses students on a mixture of multiplication and division facts for a particular group. Students take the quiz and update their *Multiplication Facts I Know* and *Division Facts I Know* charts.

The DPP for Units 7 and 8 review all five groups of facts. As students complete these items, students update their *Multiplication* and *Division Facts I Know* charts. A final DPP item in Unit 8 includes an inventory test on multiplication and division facts from all five groups. The tests help you and students assess the facts they know and those they still need to learn. During the second semester, students can use their *Triangle Flash Cards* to practice the multiplication and division facts they have not circled. The second semester's DPP includes additional math fact review, especially of the division facts. This provides further opportunities for students to strengthen their fluency with the math facts.

Content Note

The math facts program is closely linked to the recommended schedule for teaching lessons. Thus, classrooms that deviate significantly from the suggested pacing will need to make special accommodations to ensure students receive a consistent program of math facts practice and assessment throughout the year. The *Grade 5 Facts Resource Guide* outlines a schedule for math facts practice and assessment in classrooms that are moving much more slowly through lessons than recommended in the Lesson Guides. The *Grade 5 Facts Resource Guide* contains all components of the math facts program, including DPP items, flash cards, *Facts I Know* charts, and assessments.

Math Facts

Begin reviewing the multiplication and division facts for the 5s and 10s.

Homework and Practice

- Part 1 of the Home Practice reminds students to take home their flash cards for the 5s and 10s. Students should practice the multiplication and division facts they need to learn at home with a family member.

- Assign DPP Bit E which provides practice with money and DPP Task F which reviews measurement and finding a median.

Answers for the Home Practice are in the Answer Key at the end of this lesson and at the end of this unit.

Assessment

- Students use flash cards and *Facts I Know* charts to complete self assessments with the multiplication and division facts for the 5s and 10s.

- Record your observations on the *Observational Assessment Record*.

Discovery Assignment Book - page 9

Math Facts and Daily Practice and Problems

Complete items E–F in the Daily Practice and Problems.

Part 1. Multiplication Facts and Triangle Flash Cards

1. Students prepare the *Triangle Flash Cards: 5s* and *10s* found in the *Discovery Assignment Book.* Each student cuts out a complete set.
2. Students use the flash cards to quiz each other on the multiplication facts. Directions on how to use the cards are on the *Facts I Know* Activity Pages in the *Student Guide. (Question 1)*
3. As students are quizzed, they sort their cards into three piles: facts I know and can answer quickly, facts I know using a strategy, and facts I need to learn.
4. Students begin their *Multiplication Facts I Know* chart by circling the facts they know well and can answer quickly.
5. Students discuss efficient strategies to use when trying to find the answer to a multiplication fact.
6. Students list the multiplication facts they still need to practice. They take home the list of facts and the flash cards.

Part 2. Fact Families

1. Distribute a copy of *Centimeter Dot Paper* to each student. Pose the following problem: *"If a rectangle on the dot paper is made up of 30 squares and there are 5 rows of squares, how many squares are in each row?"*
2. Students create the rectangle by connecting dots on the dot paper with a ruler. Discuss how they can solve this problem using a multiplication and a division sentence—5 × ? = 30 and 30 ÷ 5 = ? Students label their rectangles with both number sentences: 5 × 6 = 30 and 30 ÷ 5 = 6.
3. Pose a similar problem: *"If a rectangle is made up of 30 squares and there are 6 rows of squares, how many squares are in each row?"*
4. Ask students to solve this problem using the dot paper. Discuss how they can solve this problem using a multiplication and a division sentence—6 × ? = 30 and 30 ÷ 6 = ? Students label their rectangles with both number sentences: 6 × 5 = 30 and 30 ÷ 6 = 5.
5. Have students cut out both rectangles and lay one directly on top of the other. Both rectangles are the same.
6. Introduce the term fact family. All four number sentences—6 × 5 = 30, 5 × 6 = 30, 30 ÷ 5 = 6, and 30 ÷ 6 = 5—represent the same rectangle. These four related facts are in the same fact family.
7. If necessary, have your students create more rectangles on *Centimeter Dot Paper* to illustrate fact families.
8. Students complete *Questions 2–11* in the Fact Families section on the *Facts I Know* Activity Pages in the *Student Guide.*

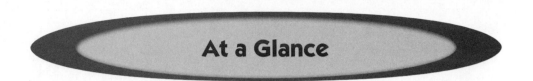

Part 3. Division Facts and Triangle Flash Cards

1. Students quiz each other on the division facts using the flash cards. Directions on how to use the cards are on the *Facts I Know* Activity Pages in the *Student Guide. (Question 12)* Student pairs first cover the numbers in squares.

2. As students are quizzed, they sort their cards into three piles: facts I know and can answer quickly, facts I know using a strategy, and facts I need to learn.

3. Students begin their *Division Facts I Know* chart by circling the facts they know well and can answer quickly.

4. Students sort the cards again. This time partners cover the numbers in circles.

5. Students update their *Division Facts I Know* chart a second time.

6. Students list the facts they need to practice.

7. Students compare their *Multiplication Facts I Know* chart to their *Division Facts I Know* chart.

8. They take home their list of facts and their flash cards to practice with a family member.

Part 4. Fact Practice in the DPP

Throughout the year, the practice and assessment of the facts continue in the DPP.

Homework

Assign Part 1 of the Home Practice that asks students to practice the math facts.

Assessment

1. Students use flash cards and *Facts I Know* charts to assess themselves on the multiplication and division facts.

2. Record your observations on the *Observational Assessment Record.*

Answer Key is on pages 64–65.

Notes:

Multiplication Facts I Know

- **Circle the facts you know well.**
- **Keep this table and use it to help you multiply.**
- **As you learn more facts, circle them too.**

×	0	1	2	3	4	5	6	7	8	9	10
0	0	0	0	0	0	0	0	0	0	0	0
1	0	1	2	3	4	5	6	7	8	9	10
2	0	2	4	6	8	10	12	14	16	18	20
3	0	3	6	9	12	15	18	21	24	27	30
4	0	4	8	12	16	20	24	28	32	36	40
5	0	5	10	15	20	25	30	35	40	45	50
6	0	6	12	18	24	30	36	42	48	54	60
7	0	7	14	21	28	35	42	49	56	63	70
8	0	8	16	24	32	40	48	56	64	72	80
9	0	9	18	27	36	45	54	63	72	81	90
10	0	10	20	30	40	50	60	70	80	90	100

Division Facts I Know

- **Circle the facts you know well.**

- **Keep this table and use it to help you divide.**

- **As you learn more facts, circle them too.**

×	0	1	2	3	4	5	6	7	8	9	10
0	0	0	0	0	0	0	0	0	0	0	0
1	0	1	2	3	4	5	6	7	8	9	10
2	0	2	4	6	8	10	12	14	16	18	20
3	0	3	6	9	12	15	18	21	24	27	30
4	0	4	8	12	16	20	24	28	32	36	40
5	0	5	10	15	20	25	30	35	40	45	50
6	0	6	12	18	24	30	36	42	48	54	60
7	0	7	14	21	28	35	42	49	56	63	70
8	0	8	16	24	32	40	48	56	64	72	80
9	0	9	18	27	36	45	54	63	72	81	90
10	0	10	20	30	40	50	60	70	80	90	100

Divisor

Centimeter Dot Paper

Facts I Know

Multiplication Facts and Triangle Flash Cards

1. Work with a partner. Use the directions below and your *Triangle Flash Cards: 5s* and *10s* to practice the multiplication facts.

   A. One partner covers the corner containing the highest number. (This number is lightly shaded on each triangle.) This number is the answer to a multiplication problem, called the **product.** The second person multiplies the two uncovered numbers which are called the **factors.**

   5 × 4 = ?

   4 × 5 = ?

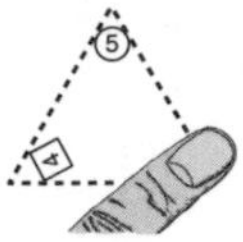

   B. Place each flash card in one of three piles: those facts you know and can answer quickly, those you can figure out with a strategy, and those you need to learn.

   C. Begin your *Multiplication Facts I Know* chart. Circle those facts you know well and can answer quickly.

   For example, Felicia looked through the pile of facts she knew well and answered quickly. Felicia knew that 5 × 4 = 20 and 4 × 5 = 20. She circled two 20s on the chart. Look for the two other 20s on the chart. Why didn't Felicia circle these as well?

   D. Discuss how you can figure out facts you don't recall right away. Share your strategies with your partner.

   E. Practice the last two piles at home for homework—the facts you can figure out with a strategy and those you need to learn. Make a list of those facts you need to practice.

Multiplication Facts I Know

×	0	1	2	3	4	5	6	7	8	9	10
0	0	0	0	0	0	0	0	0	0	0	0
1	0	1	2	3	4	5	6	7	8	9	10
2	0	2	4	6	8	10	12	14	16	18	20
3	0	3	6	9	12	15	18	21	24	27	30
4	0	4	8	12	16	20	24	28	32	36	40
5	0	5	10	15	20	25	30	35	40	45	50
6	0	6	12	18	24	30	36	42	48	54	60
7	0	7	14	21	28	35	42	49	56	63	70
8	0	8	16	24	32	40	48	56	64	72	80
9	0	9	18	27	36	45	54	63	72	81	90
10	0	10	20	30	40	50	60	70	80	90	100

Facts I Know SG • Grade 5 • Unit 2 • Lesson 2 35

***Student Guide* - page 35**

Fact Families

2. The picture below models the following problem: *if a rectangle has a total of 20 squares organized in 4 rows, how many squares are in each row?*

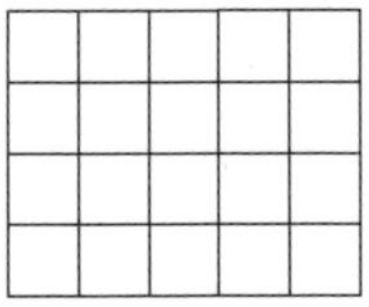

   What division sentence describes this problem?

3. The picture below models the following problem: *if a rectangle has a total of 20 squares organized in 5 rows, how many squares are in each row?*

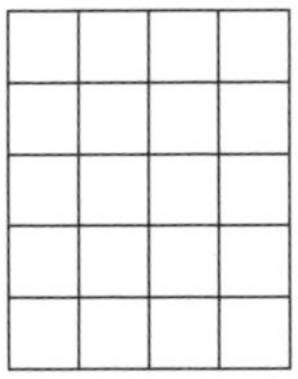

   What division sentence describes this problem?

4. What do you notice about the rectangles in Questions 2 and 3? (If you need to, draw both of these rectangles on a piece of *Dot Paper*. Cut them out and lay one on top of the other.)

5. What two multiplication sentences describe the two rectangles in Questions 2 and 3?

The four facts: 4 × 5 = 20
5 × 4 = 20
20 ÷ 4 = 5
and 20 ÷ 5 = 4 are related facts. We say they are in the same **fact family.**

36 SG • Grade 5 • Unit 2 • Lesson 2 Facts I Know

***Student Guide* - page 36**

Student Guide (pp. 35–36)

Facts I Know

1.*

2. 20 ÷ 4 = 5

3. 20 ÷ 5 = 4

4. The rectangles are the same. If you cut one out and turn it around, you can lay it directly on top of the other.

5. 4 × 5 = 20 and 5 × 4 = 20

*Answers and/or discussion are included in the Lesson Guide.

Student Guide (pp. 37–38)

6. A. 10; 10; $10 \div 2 = 5$; $10 \div 5 = 2$

   B. 30; 30; $30 \div 3 = 10$; $30 \div 10 = 3$

   C. 50; 5; $5 \times 10 = 50$; $50 \div 5 = 10$

   D. 30; 6; $5 \times 6 = 30$; $30 \div 6 = 5$

7. A. 40; $40 \div 5 = 8$; $40 \div 8 = 5$; $5 \times 8 = 40$

   B. 70; $70 \div 10 = 7$; $70 \div 7 = 10$;
      $10 \times 7 = 70$

   C. $90 \div 10 = 9$; $9 \times 10 = 90$; $90 \div 9 = 10$;
      $10 \times 9 = 90$

   D. $5 \times 9 = 45$; $45 \div 5 = 9$; $5 \times 9 = 45$;
      $45 \div 9 = 5$

8. 25; $25 \div 5 = 5$; No.*

9. 100; $100 \div 10 = 10$; No.*

10. There are only two facts in the fact families for square numbers.*

11. A. 60; $6 \times 10 = 60$; $60 \div 6 = 10$;
      $60 \div 10 = 6$

   B. 2; $20 \div 2 = 10$; $2 \times 10 = 20$; $10 \times 2 = 20$

   C. 35; $5 \times 7 = 35$; $35 \div 7 = 5$; $35 \div 5 = 7$

   D. 10; $80 \div 10 = 8$; $8 \times 10 = 80$;
      $10 \times 8 = 80$

   E. 5; $15 \div 5 = 3$; $3 \times 5 = 15$; $5 \times 3 = 15$

   F. 40; $10 \times 4 = 40$; $40 \div 4 = 10$;
      $40 \div 10 = 4$

   G. 15; $5 \times 3 = 15$; $15 \div 3 = 5$; $15 \div 5 = 3$

   H. 5; $10 \div 5 = 2$; $2 \times 5 = 10$; $5 \times 2 = 10$

12. *

13. Answers will vary.*

---

6. Solve each pair of related facts. Name two other facts in the same fact family.

   A. $5 \times 2 = ?$ and $2 \times 5 = ?$ **B.** $10 \times 3 = ?$ and $3 \times 10 = ?$

   C. $10 \times 5 = ?$ and $50 \div 10 = ?$ **D.** $6 \times 5 = ?$ and $30 \div 5 = ?$

7. Write the complete number sentence for each related fact.

   A. $8 \times 5 =$ _____   **B.** $7 \times 10 =$ _____

      _____ $\div 5 =$ _____   _____ $\div$ _____ $= 7$

      _____ $\div 8 =$ _____   _____ $\div 7 =$ _____

      $5 \times$ _____ $=$ _____ $10 \times$ _____ $=$ _____

   C. $90 \div$ _____ $= 9$ **D.** $5 \times$ ___ $= 45$

      _____ $\times 10 =$ _____ $45 \div$ _____ $=$ _____

      _____ $\div 9 =$ _____   _____ $\times 9 =$ _____

      _____ $\times 9 =$ _____ $45 \div$ _____ $=$ _____

8. What is 5×5? Name a related fact for 5×5. Is there more than one?

9. What is 10×10? Name a related fact for 10×10. Is there more than one?

10. The numbers 25 and 100 are square numbers. How are the fact families for the square numbers different from other fact families?

11. Solve the given fact. Then name other facts in the same fact family.

   A. $10 \times 6 = ?$ **B.** $20 \div 10 = ?$ **C.** $7 \times 5 = ?$ **D.** $80 \div 8 = ?$

   E. $15 \div 3 = ?$ **F.** $4 \times 10 = ?$ **G.** $3 \times 5 = ?$ **H.** $10 \div 2 = ?$

Division Facts and Triangle Flash Cards

12. With a partner, use the directions below and your *Triangle Flash Cards: 5s* and *10s* to practice the division facts.

   A. One partner covers the number in the square. This number will be the answer to a division problem, called the **quotient.** The number in the circle is the **divisor.** The second person solves a division fact with the two uncovered numbers as shown.

$20 \div 5 = ?$

Facts I Know   SG • Grade 5 • Unit 2 • Lesson 2   **37**

Student Guide - page 37

B. Place each flash card in one of three piles: those facts you know well and can answer quickly, those you can figure out with a strategy, and those you need to learn.

C. Begin your *Division Facts I Know* chart. Circle the facts you know well and can answer quickly.

For example, Edward knew $20 \div 5 = 4$. So Edward circled the 20 in the row for a divisor of 5.

Division Facts I Know

×	0	1	2	3	4	5	6	7	8	9	10
0	0	0	0	0	0	0	0	0	0	0	0
1	0	1	2	3	4	5	6	7	8	9	10
2	0	2	4	6	8	10	12	14	16	18	20
3	0	3	6	9	12	15	18	21	24	27	30
4	0	4	8	12	16	20	24	28	32	36	40
5	0	5	10	15	(20)	25	30	35	40	45	50
6	0	6	12	18	24	30	36	42	48	54	60
7	0	7	14	21	28	35	42	49	56	63	70
8	0	8	16	24	32	40	48	56	64	72	80
9	0	9	18	27	36	45	54	63	72	81	90
10	0	10	20	30	40	50	60	70	80	90	100

Divisor

D. Sort the cards again. This time your partner covers the number in the circle. The number in the square is now the divisor. Solve a division fact with the two uncovered numbers.

E. Update your *Division Facts I Know* chart. Circle the facts you know well and can answer quickly.

$20 \div 4 = ?$

F. Discuss how you can figure out facts you don't recall right away. Share your strategies with your partner.

G. Practice the last two piles at home for homework—the facts you can figure out with a strategy and those you need to learn. Make a list of these facts.

13. Compare your *Multiplication Facts I Know* chart to your *Division Facts I Know* chart. Look for facts in the same fact family. Do you know any complete fact families? Which family or families? Explain.

You will continue to use *Triangle Flash Cards* to study other groups of facts. You will be reminded to update your *Multiplication* and *Division Facts I Know* charts. If you know one or two of the facts in a fact family, use those facts to help you learn the others.

38   SG • Grade 5 • Unit 2 • Lesson 2   Facts I Know

Student Guide - page 38

*Answers and/or discussion are included in the Lesson Guide.

Facts Distribution

Multiplication and Division: 2s and 3s • Weeks 6–8

Math Facts Groups	Weeks	Daily Practice and Problems	Home Practice	Triangle Flash Cards	Facts Quizzes and Tests
Multiplication and Division: 2s and 3s	6–8	Unit 3: items 3B, 3C, 3D, 3E, 3I, 3K, 3O & 3U	Unit 3 Part 1	*Triangle Flash Cards: 2s and 3s*	DPP item 3U is a quiz on the 2s and 3s. The *Multiplication* and *Division Facts I Know* charts are updated.

Students may solve the items individually, in groups, or as a class. The items may also be assigned for homework. The DPPs are also available on the Teacher Resource CD.

Student Questions	Teacher Notes

 Multiplication and Division Facts: 2s and 3s

With a partner, use your *Triangle Flash Cards* to quiz each other on the multiplication and division facts for the 2s and 3s. Follow the directions in the *Student Guide* for Unit 2 Lesson 2 *Facts I Know.*

As your partner quizzes you on the multiplication facts, separate the facts into three piles: those facts you know and can answer quickly, those you can figure out with a strategy, and those you need to learn. Practice any facts for the 2s and 3s that are in the last two piles. List these facts so you can practice them at home. Repeat the process for the division facts.

Circle all the facts you know and can answer quickly on your *Multiplication* and *Division Facts I Know* charts.

TIMS Bit

The *Triangle Flash Cards: 2s* are in the *Discovery Assignment Book* following the Home Practice. Blackline masters of all the flash cards, organized by group, are in Section 7. Part 1 of the Home Practice reminds students to take home the list of 2s and 3s they need to study as well as their flash cards.

The *Multiplication* and *Division Facts I Know* charts were distributed in Unit 2 Lesson 2. See that Lesson Guide for more information.

Inform students when you will give the quiz on these facts. This quiz, which assesses students on multiplication and division facts for the 2s and 3s, appears in DPP item 3U.

3C Multiplying by 10s

A. $30 \times 20 =$

B. $80 \times 30 =$

C. $200 \times 60 =$

D. $50 \times 300 =$

E. $1000 \times 30 =$

F. $900 \times 200 =$

G. $6000 \times 300 =$

H. $20 \times 200 =$

I. $7000 \times 3 =$

TIMS Task

A. 600   B. 2400

C. 12,000   D. 15,000

E. 30,000   F. 180,000

G. 1,800,000 H. 4000

I. 21,000

3D Bikes and Trikes

There are some bicycles and some tricycles in the TIMS warehouse. The total number of wheels is 35.

1. How many bikes and how many trikes might be in the TIMS warehouse? (Give several answers to this problem.)

2. What is the fewest number of bikes that can be in the warehouse? Then how many trikes will there be?

3. What is the fewest number of trikes that can be in the warehouse? Then how many bikes will there be?

4. If the warehouse has a total of 15 bikes and trikes altogether, how many of each are in the warehouse?

5. If the number of bikes and trikes is the same, how many of each are in the warehouse?

TIMS Bit

1. Some students may get only one answer for the problem. Others may be able to make a table and exhaust the possibilities. One possible answer is: 5 trikes ($5 \times 3 = 15$ wheels) and 10 bikes ($10 \times 2 = 20$ wheels).

2. If there is only one bike, then 35 wheels – 2 wheels = 33 wheels left. 33 wheels ÷ 3 wheels each = 11 trikes.

3. If there is only one trike, then 35 wheels – 3 wheels = 32 wheels left. 32 wheels ÷ 2 wheels each = 16 bikes.

4. 5 trikes and 10 bikes ($5 \times 3 + 10 \times 2 = 35$ wheels)

5. 7 trikes and 7 bikes ($7 \times 3 + 7 \times 2 = 35$ wheels)

3E **Fact Families for × and ÷**

Solve each pair of related facts. Then name two other facts in the same fact family.

A. $4 \times 2 = ?$ and $8 \div 2 = ?$

B. $9 \times 3 = ?$ and $27 \div 3 = ?$

C. $3 \times 5 = ?$ and $15 \div 3 = ?$

D. $2 \times 8 = ?$ and $16 \div 8 = ?$

E. $10 \times 2 = ?$ and $20 \div 10 = ?$

F. $4 \times 3 = ?$ and $12 \div 3 = ?$

G. $7 \times 2 = ?$ and $14 \div 2 = ?$

H. $3 \times 6 = ?$ and $18 \div 3 = ?$

TIMS Bit

A. 8; 4; $2 \times 4 = 8$; $8 \div 4 = 2$

B. 27; 9; $3 \times 9 = 27$; $27 \div 9 = 3$

C. 15; 5; $5 \times 3 = 15$; $15 \div 5 = 3$

D. 16; 2; $8 \times 2 = 16$; $16 \div 2 = 8$

E. 20; 2; $2 \times 10 = 20$; $20 \div 2 = 10$

F. 12; 4; $3 \times 4 = 12$; $12 \div 4 = 3$

G. 14; 7; $2 \times 7 = 14$; $14 \div 7 = 2$

H. 18; 6; $6 \times 3 = 18$; $18 \div 6 = 3$

3I **Mixed Numbers and Improper Fractions**

1. Write a whole number or a mixed number for each improper fraction.

   A. $\frac{15}{4}$ B. $\frac{24}{8}$ C. $\frac{29}{3}$

2. Write an improper fraction for each mixed number.

   A. $6\frac{2}{3}$ B. $9\frac{1}{2}$ C. $5\frac{1}{3}$

TIMS Task

1. A. $3\frac{3}{4}$

   B. 3

   C. $9\frac{2}{3}$

2. A. $\frac{20}{3}$

   B. $\frac{19}{2}$

   C. $\frac{16}{3}$

Student Questions	Teacher Notes

 Fact Families for × and ÷

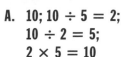 **TIMS Task**

Complete the number sentences for the related facts.

A. $5 \times 2 =$ ___

___ $\div 5 =$ ___

___ $\div 2 =$ ___

$2 \times$ ___ $=$ ___

B. $8 \times 3 =$ ___

___ $\div$ ___ $= 8$

___ $\div 8 =$ ___

___ $\times 8 =$ ___

C. $18 \div 2 =$ ___

___ $\times 2 =$ ___

$18 \div$ ___ $=$ ___

$2 \times$ ___ $=$ ___

D. $3 \times$ ___ $= 6$

$6 \div$ ___ $=$ ___

$6 \div$ ___ $=$ ___

___ $\times 3 =$ ___

A. 10; 10 ÷ 5 = 2;
10 ÷ 2 = 5;
2 × 5 = 10

B. 24; 24 ÷ 3 = 8;
24 ÷ 8 = 3;
3 × 8 = 24

C. 9; 9 × 2 = 18;
18 ÷ 9 = 2;
2 × 9 = 18

D. 2; 6 ÷ 2 = 3 or
6 ÷ 3 = 2;
2 × 3 = 6

---

30 **Fact Families for × and ÷**

 TIMS Bit

Complete the number sentences for the related facts.

A. $3 \times 10 =$ ___

___ $\div 3 =$ ___

___ $\div 10 =$ ___

___ $\times 3 =$ ___

B. $3 \times 7 =$ ___

___ $\div 7 =$ ___

___ $\div 3 =$ ___

$7 \times$ ___ $=$ ___

C. $2 \times 2 =$ ___

___ $\div 2 =$ ___

D. $12 \div 6 =$ ___

___ $\times 6 =$ ___

$12 \div$ ___ $=$ ___

___ $\times 2 =$ ___

E. $3 \times$ ___ $= 9$

$9 \div$ ___ $=$ ___

A. 30; 30 ÷ 3 = 10;
30 ÷ 10 = 3;
10 × 3 = 30

B. 21; 21 ÷ 7 = 3;
21 ÷ 3 = 7;
7 × 3 = 21

C. 4; 4 ÷ 2 = 2

D. 2; 2 × 6 = 12;
12 ÷ 2 = 6;
6 × 2 = 12

E. 3 × 3 = 9;
9 ÷ 3 = 3

Quiz: 2s and 3s

A. $3 \times 5 =$

B. $14 \div 2 =$

C. $18 \div 3 =$

D. $3 \times 10 =$

E. $2 \times 2 =$

F. $7 \times 3 =$

G. $12 \div 6 =$

H. $8 \div 4 =$

I. $12 \div 4 =$

J. $24 \div 3 =$

K. $9 \div 3 =$

L. $2 \times 9 =$

M. $9 \times 3 =$

N. $5 \times 2 =$

O. $16 \div 8 =$

P. $3 \times 2 =$

Q. $20 \div 2 =$

TIMS Bit

We recommend 5 minutes for this quiz. Allow students to change pens after the time is up and complete the remaining problems in a different color. After students take the test, have them update their *Multiplication Facts I Know* and *Division Facts I Know* charts.

Unit 3 Home Practice

PART 1 Triangle Flash Cards: 2s and 3s

Study for the quiz on the multiplication and division facts for the 2s and 3s. Take home your *Triangle Flash Cards: 2s* and *3s* and your list of facts you need to study.

Ask a family member to choose one flash card at a time. To quiz you on a multiplication fact, he or she should cover the corner containing the highest number. Multiply the two uncovered numbers.

To quiz you on a division fact, your partner can cover one of the smaller numbers. One of the smaller numbers on each card is circled. The other has a square around it. Use the two uncovered numbers to solve a division fact.

Now mix up the multiplication and division facts. Your partner should sometimes cover the highest number, sometimes cover the circled number, and sometimes cover the number in the square.

Your teacher will tell you when the quiz on the 2s and 3s will be given.

Facts Distribution

Multiplication and Division: Square Numbers • Weeks 9–12

Math Facts Groups	Weeks	Daily Practice and Problems	Home Practice	Triangle Flash Cards	Facts Quizzes and Tests
Multiplication and Division: Square Numbers	9–12	Unit 4: items 4B, 4E, 4I, 4K, 4M, 4S, 4Z & 4AA	Unit 4 Part 1	*Triangle Flash Cards: Square Numbers*	DPP item 4AA is a quiz on the square numbers. The *Multiplication* and *Division Facts I Know* charts are updated.

Weeks 9–12

 **Daily Practice and Problems**

Students may solve the items individually, in groups, or as a class. The items may also be assigned for homework. The DPPs are also available on the Teacher Resource CD.

Student Questions	Teacher Notes

 Multiplication and Division Facts: Square Numbers

With a partner, use your *Triangle Flash Cards* to quiz each other on the multiplication and division facts for the square numbers. Follow the directions in the *Student Guide* for Unit 2 Lesson 2 *Facts I Know.*

As your partner quizzes you on the multiplication facts, separate the facts into three piles: those facts you know and can answer quickly, those you can figure out with a strategy, and those you need to learn. Practice any facts for the square numbers in the last two piles. List these facts so you can practice them at home. Repeat the process for the division facts.

Circle all the facts you know and can answer quickly on your *Multiplication* and *Division Facts I Know* charts. As you circle the facts for the square numbers on your chart, what patterns do you see?

TIMS Task

The *Triangle Flash Cards: Square Numbers* are in the *Discovery Assignment Book* following the Home Practice. Blackline masters of all the flash cards, organized by group, are in Section 7. Part 1 of the Home Practice reminds students to take home the list of square numbers they need to study as well as their flash cards.

The *Multiplication* and *Division Facts I Know* charts were distributed in Unit 2 Lesson 2. As students fill in their charts, they should see that the products for the square numbers lie on the diagonal that divides the chart in half. Point out to students that they need to circle only one fact since the turn-around fact is the same.

Inform students when you will give the quiz on these facts. The quiz appears in DPP item 4AA.

Student Questions	Teacher Notes

4E **Practicing the Facts**

A. $3 \times 3 =$

B. $8 \times 8 =$

C. $6 \times 6 =$

D. $5 \times 5 =$

E. $10 \times 10 =$

F. $2 \times 2 =$

G. $4 \times 4 =$

H. $7 \times 7 =$

I. $9 \times 9 =$

TIMS Bit

A. 9   B. 64

C. 36   D. 25

E. 100   F. 4

G. 16   H. 49

I. 81

4I **Fact Families for the Square Numbers**

The square numbers only have two facts in each fact family.

For example, the following two facts are in the same fact family.

$$2 \times 2 = 4 \text{ and } 4 \div 2 = 2$$

Solve the fact. Then name the second fact in the same fact family.

A. $9 \times 9 = ?$

B. $5 \times 5 = ?$

C. $7 \times 7 = ?$

D. $8 \times 8 = ?$

E. $10 \times 10 = ?$

F. $3 \times 3 = ?$

G. $6 \times 6 = ?$

H. $4 \times 4 = ?$

TIMS Bit

A. $81; 81 \div 9 = 9$

B. $25; 25 \div 5 = 5$

C. $49; 49 \div 7 = 7$

D. $64; 64 \div 8 = 8$

E. $100; 100 \div 10 = 10$

F. $9; 9 \div 3 = 3$

G. $36; 36 \div 6 = 6$

H. $16; 16 \div 4 = 4$

4K **Fact Families for × and ÷**

Complete the number sentences for the related facts.

A. $2 \times 2 =$ ___   B. $8 \times 8 =$ ___

___ $\div 2 =$ ___   ___ $\div$ ___ $= 8$

C. $36 \div 6 =$ ___   D. $10 \times$ ___ $= 100$

___ $\times 6 =$ ___ $100 \div$ ___ $=$ ___

TIMS Bit

A. 4; $4 \div 2 = 2$

B. 64; $64 \div 8 = 8$

C. 6; $6 \times 6 = 36$

D. 10; $100 \div 10 = 10$

4M **Fact Families for × and ÷**

Complete the number sentences for the related facts.

A. $3 \times 3 =$ ___   B. $7 \times 7 =$ ___

___ $\div 3 =$ ___   ___ $\div 7 =$ ___

C. $9 \times 9 =$ ___   D. $25 \div 5 =$ ___

___ $\div 9 =$ ___   ___ $\times 5 =$ ___

E. $4 \times 4 =$ ___

___ $\div$ ___ $= 4$

TIMS Bit

A. 9; $9 \div 3 = 3$

B. 49; $49 \div 7 = 7$

C. 81; $81 \div 9 = 9$

D. 5; $5 \times 5 = 25$

E. 16; $16 \div 4 = 4$

4S **Multiplying and Dividing by Multiples of 10**

A. $800 \times 80 =$ B. $25,000 \div 50 =$

C. $4900 \div 7 =$ D. $10,000 \div 10 =$

E. $40 \times 400 =$ F. $8100 \div 90 =$

TIMS Bit

A. 64,000

B. 500

C. 700

D. 1000

E. 16,000

F. 90

Order of Operations

Solve each pair of problems and compare their answers.

A. $5 \times (7 - 2) =$

   $5 \times 7 - 2 =$

B. $30 - 3 \times 7 =$

   $(30 - 3) \times 7 =$

C. $18 \div 2 \times 3 =$

   $18 \div (2 \times 3) =$

D. $(4 + 3) \times (8 + 2) =$

   $4 + 3 \times 8 + 2 =$

TIMS Task

Students should see that using parentheses changes the answers.

A. 25; 33

B. 9; 189

C. 27; 3

D. 70; 30

4AA **Quiz: Square Numbers**

A. $5 \times 5 =$ B. $4 \div 2 =$

C. $81 \div 9 =$ D. $10 \times 10 =$

E. $8 \times 8 =$ F. $16 \div 4 =$

G. $9 \div 3 =$ H. $6 \times 6 =$

I. $49 \div 7 =$

TIMS Bit

We recommend 2 minutes for this quiz. Allow students to change pens after the time is up and complete the remaining problems in a different color. After students take the quiz, have them update their *Multiplication Facts I Know* and *Division Facts I Know* charts.

Unit 4 Home Practice

Study for the quiz on the multiplication and division facts for the square numbers. Take home your *Triangle Flash Cards: Square Numbers* and your list of facts you need to study.

To quiz a multiplication fact, cover the corner containing the highest number. Multiply the two uncovered numbers.

To quiz a division fact, cover one of the smaller numbers. Use the two uncovered numbers to solve a division fact.

Mix up the multiplication and division facts. Sometimes cover the highest number and sometimes cover a smaller number.

Your teacher will tell you when the quiz on the square numbers will be given.

Section 5

Facts Distribution
Multiplication and Division: 9s •
Weeks 13–15

Math Facts Groups	Weeks	Daily Practice and Problems	Home Practice	Triangle Flash Cards	Facts Quizzes and Tests
Multiplication and Division: 9s	13–15	Unit 5: items 5B, 5C, 5D, 5E, 5I, 5K, 5O & 5S	Unit 5 Part 1	*Triangle Flash Cards: 9s*	DPP item 5S is a quiz on the 9s. The *Multiplication* and *Division Facts I Know* charts are updated.

 **Daily Practice and Problems**

Students may solve the items individually, in groups, or as a class. The items may also be assigned for homework. The DPPs are also available on the Teacher Resource CD.

Student Questions	Teacher Notes

 Multiplication and Division Facts: 9s

With a partner, use your *Triangle Flash Cards* to quiz each other on the multiplication and division facts for the 9s. Follow the directions in the *Student Guide* for Unit 2 Lesson 2 *Facts I Know.*

As your partner quizzes you on the multiplication facts, separate the facts into three piles: those facts you know and can answer quickly, those you can figure out with a strategy, and those you need to learn. Practice any facts for the 9s in the last two piles. List these facts so you can practice them at home. Repeat the process for the division facts.

Circle all the facts you know and can answer quickly on your *Multiplication* and *Division Facts I Know* charts.

TIMS Task

The *Triangle Flash Cards: 9s* are in the *Discovery Assignment Book* following the Home Practice. Blackline masters of all the flash cards, organized by group, are in Section 7. Part 1 of the Home Practice reminds students to take home the list of 9s they need to study as well as their flash cards.

The *Multiplication* and *Division Facts I Know* charts were distributed in the *Unit Resource Guide* for Unit 2 Lesson 2. See that Lesson Guide for more information.

Inform students when you will give the quiz on these facts. This assessment appears in DPP item 5S.

5C Order of Operations

A. $20 \div 5 \times 9 =$ B. $18 - 3 \times 3 =$

C. $3 + 9 \times 3 =$ D. $(6 + 3) \times 8 =$

TIMS Bit

A. 36
B. 9
C. 30
D. 72

5D How Many Answers?

Leaving the numbers in the order given, use operations ($+$, $-$, $\times$, $\div$) and parentheses to get as many different answers as you can. You may use an operation more than once.

Example: 2   4   6

$$2 + 4 \times 6 = 26$$

$$(2 + 4) \times 6 = 36$$

$$(2 + 4) \div 6 = 1$$

A. 25   5   10

B. 30   6   2

Only whole numbers are allowed at each step. For example, $2 \div 4 + 6$ is not allowed, since $2 \div 4 = \frac{1}{2}$.

TIMS Challenge

A. Some possibilities are:
$25 \div 5 \times 10 = 50$;
$(25 + 5) \div 10 = 3$;
$(25 - 5) \div 10 = 2$

B. Some possibilities are:
$30 \div 6 + 2 = 7$;
$30 \times 6 \div 2 = 90$;
$(30 - 6) \times 2 = 48$;
$30 - 6 \times 2 = 18$;
$30 + 6 - 2 = 34$

5E Multiplying by 10s

A. $30 \times 90 =$ B. $80 \times 90 =$

C. $900 \times 60 =$ D. $50 \times 900 =$

E. $1000 \times 90 =$ F. $900 \times 200 =$

G. $4000 \times 900 =$ H. $70 \times 900 =$

I. $9000 \times 9 =$

TIMS Bit

A. 2700   B. 7200

C. 54,000   D. 45,000

E. 90,000   F. 180,000

G. 3,600,000 H. 63,000

I. 81,000

Student Questions	Teacher Notes

 Fact Families for × and ÷

Solve each pair of related facts. Then name two other facts in the same fact family.

A. $9 \times 2 = ?$ and $18 \div 2 = ?$

B. $5 \times 9 = ?$ and $45 \div 9 = ?$

C. $7 \times 9 = ?$ and $63 \div 7 = ?$

D. $9 \times 8 = ?$ and $72 \div 9 = ?$

E. $10 \times 9 = ?$ and $90 \div 10 = ?$

F. $3 \times 9 = ?$ and $27 \div 3 = ?$

G. $9 \times 6 = ?$ and $54 \div 6 = ?$

H. $9 \times 4 = ?$ and $36 \div 9 = ?$

A. 18; 9; $2 \times 9 = 18$;
$18 \div 9 = 2$

B. 45; 5; $9 \times 5 = 45$;
$45 \div 5 = 9$

C. 63; 9; $9 \times 7 = 63$;
$63 \div 9 = 7$

D. 72; 8; $8 \times 9 = 72$;
$72 \div 8 = 9$

E. 90; 9; $9 \times 10 = 90$;
$90 \div 9 = 10$

F. 27; 9; $9 \times 3 = 27$;
$27 \div 9 = 3$

G. 54; 9; $6 \times 9 = 54$;
$54 \div 9 = 6$

H. 36; 4; $4 \times 9 = 36$;
$36 \div 4 = 9$

5K **Fact Families for × and ÷**

TIMS Bit

Complete the number sentences for the related facts.

A. $9 \times 2 =$ ___

___ $\div\ 9 =$ ___

___ $\div\ 2 =$ ___

$2 \times$ ___ $=$ ___

B. $8 \times 9 =$ ___

___ $\div$ ___ $= 8$

___ $\div\ 8 =$ ___

___ $\times\ 8 =$ ___

C. $36 \div 4 =$ ___

___ $\times\ 4 =$ ___

$36 \div$ ___ $=$ ___

$4 \times$ ___ $=$ ___

D. $10 \times$ ___ $= 90$

$90 \div$ ___ $=$ ___

$90 \div$ ___ $=$ ___

___ $\times\ 10 =$ ___

A. 18; $18 \div 9 = 2$;
$18 \div 2 = 9$;
$2 \times 9 = 18$

B. 72; $72 \div 9 = 8$;
$72 \div 8 = 9$;
$9 \times 8 = 72$

C. 9; $9 \times 4 = 36$;
$36 \div 9 = 4$;
$4 \times 9 = 36$

D. 9; $90 \div 9 = 10$;
$90 \div 10 = 9$;
$9 \times 10 = 90$

50 **Fact Families for × and ÷**

Complete the number sentences for the related facts.

A. 3 × 9 = ___

   ___ ÷ 3 = ___

   ___ ÷ 9 = ___

   ___ × 3 = ___

B. 9 × 7 = ___

   ___ ÷ 7 = ___

   ___ ÷ 9 = ___

   7 × ___ = ___

C. 9 × 9 = ___

   ___ ÷ 9 = ___

D. 54 ÷ 6 = ___

   ___ × 6 = ___

   54 ÷ ___ = ___

   ___ × 9 = ___

E. 9 × 5 = ___

   ___ ÷ 9 = ___

   ___ ÷ 5 = ___

   ___ × 9 = ___

TIMS Bit

A. 27; 27 ÷ 3 = 9;
    27 ÷ 9 = 3;
    9 × 3 = 27

B. 63; 63 ÷ 7 = 9;
    63 ÷ 9 = 7;
    7 × 9 = 63

C. 81; 81 ÷ 9 = 9

D. 9; 9 × 6 = 54;
    54 ÷ 9 = 6;
    6 × 9 = 54

E. 45; 45 ÷ 9 = 5;
    45 ÷ 5 = 9;
    5 × 9 = 45

5S **Quiz: 9s**

A. 9 × 5 =

C. 27 ÷ 9 =

E. 8 × 9 =

G. 81 ÷ 9 =

I. 54 ÷ 6 =

B. 18 ÷ 2 =

D. 9 × 10 =

F. 4 × 9 =

H. 7 × 9 =

TIMS Bit

We recommend 2 minutes for this quiz. Allow students to change pens after the time is up and complete the remaining problems in a different color. Have them update their *Multiplication Facts I Know* and *Division Facts I Know* charts.

Unit 5 Home Practice

Triangle Flash Cards: 9s

Study for the quiz on the multiplication and division facts for the nines. Take home your *Triangle Flash Cards: 9s* and your list of facts you need to study.

Ask a family member to choose one flash card at a time. To quiz you on a multiplication fact, he or she should cover the corner containing the highest number. Multiply the two uncovered numbers.

To quiz you on a division fact, your family member can cover one of the smaller numbers. One of the smaller numbers is circled. The other has a square around it. Use the two uncovered numbers to solve a division fact.

Ask your family member to mix up the multiplication and division facts. He or she should sometimes cover the highest number, sometimes cover the circled number, and sometimes cover the number in the square.

Your teacher will tell you when the quiz on the 9s will be given.

Facts Distribution
Multiplication and Division:
The Last Six Facts • Weeks 16–18

Math Facts Groups	Weeks	Daily Practice and Problems	Home Practice	Triangle Flash Cards	Facts Quizzes and Tests
Multiplication and Division: The Last Six Facts	16–18	Unit 6: items 6B, 6D, 6E, 6G, 6K, 6O, 6P & 6Q	Unit 6 Part 1	*Triangle Flash Cards: Last Six Facts*	DPP item 6Q is a quiz on the last six facts. The *Multiplication* and *Division Facts I Know* charts are updated.

Students may solve the items individually, in groups, or as a class. The items may also be assigned for homework. The DPPs are also available on the Teacher Resource CD.

Student Questions	**Teacher Notes**

 Multiplication and Division Facts: The Last Six Facts

With a partner, use your *Triangle Flash Cards* to quiz each other on the last six facts. Follow the directions in the *Student Guide* for Unit 2 Lesson 2.

As your partner quizzes you on the multiplication facts, separate the facts into three piles: those facts you know and can answer quickly, those you can figure out with a strategy, and those you need to learn. Practice the facts in the last two piles. List these facts so you can practice them at home. Repeat the process for the division facts.

Circle all the facts you know and can answer quickly on your *Multiplication* and *Division Facts I Know* charts.

TIMS Task

The *Triangle Flash Cards: Last Six Facts* follow the Home Practice in the *Discovery Assignment Book*. Blackline masters of all the flash cards, organized by group, are in Section 7. Part 1 of the Home Practice reminds students to take home the list of facts they need to study as well as their flash cards.

The *Multiplication* and *Division Facts I Know* charts were distributed in the *Unit Resource Guide* for Unit 2 Lesson 2. See the Lesson Guide for more information.

Inform students when you will give the quiz on these facts. This quiz appears in DPP item 6Q.

6D Choose Your Number Sentence

TIMS Challenge

One example is provided for each.

Use each number once in any order with any operation sign (−, +, ×, ÷) to find the given answer. Remember, you can use parentheses, too.

A. $(6 \times 3 - 15) \times 2 = 6$

B. $15 - 6 \div 2 \div 3 = 14$

C. $15 \times (6 - 3 - 2) = 15$

D. $6 \times 2 - 15 \div 3 = 7$

E. $15 - (6 \times 2 + 3) = 0$

F. $15 \times 6 \times 3 \times 2 = 540$

| 6 | 3 | 15 | 2 |

A. _____ = 6

B. _____ = 14

C. _____ = 15

D. _____ = 7

E. Write a number sentence using each of these numbers once to get the smallest possible (whole number) answer.

F. Write a number sentence to give you the largest possible answer.

6E Practice with the Facts

TIMS Bit

A. $4 \times 8 =$ B. $7 \times 6 =$

C. $6 \times 4 =$ D. $8 \times 6 =$

E. $4 \times 7 =$ F. $8 \times 7 =$

G. Describe a strategy for finding 8×7.

A. 32   B. 42

C. 24   D. 48

E. 28   F. 56

G. $8 \times 7 = 8 \times 5 + 8 \times 2 =$
40 + 16 = 56

Strategies will vary.

Student Questions	Teacher Notes

 Fact Families for × and ÷

Complete the number sentences for the related facts.

A. $4 \times 7 = \underline{\quad}$

$\underline{\quad} \div 4 = \underline{\quad}$

$\underline{\quad} \div 7 = \underline{\quad}$

$\underline{\quad} \times 4 = \underline{\quad}$

B. $8 \times 6 = \underline{\quad}$

$\underline{\quad} \div 8 = \underline{\quad}$

$\underline{\quad} \div 6 = \underline{\quad}$

$6 \times \underline{\quad} = \underline{\quad}$

C. $6 \times 7 = \underline{\quad}$

$\underline{\quad} \div 6 = \underline{\quad}$

$\underline{\quad} \div 7 = \underline{\quad}$

$\underline{\quad} \times 6 = \underline{\quad}$

D. $24 \div 6 = \underline{\quad}$

$\underline{\quad} \times 6 = \underline{\quad}$

$24 \div \underline{\quad} = \underline{\quad}$

$\underline{\quad} \times 4 = \underline{\quad}$

E. $8 \times 7 = \underline{\quad}$

$\underline{\quad} \div 8 = \underline{\quad}$

$\underline{\quad} \div 7 = \underline{\quad}$

$\underline{\quad} \times 8 = \underline{\quad}$

F. $32 \div 8 = \underline{\quad}$

$4 \times \underline{\quad} = \underline{\quad}$

$\underline{\quad} \div 4 = \underline{\quad}$

$\underline{\quad} \times 4 = \underline{\quad}$

A. 28; $28 \div 4 = 7$;
$28 \div 7 = 4$;
$7 \times 4 = 28$

B. 48; $48 \div 8 = 6$;
$48 \div 6 = 8$;
$6 \times 8 = 48$

C. 42; $42 \div 6 = 7$;
$42 \div 7 = 6$;
$7 \times 6 = 42$

D. 4; $4 \times 6 = 24$;
$24 \div 4 = 6$;
$6 \times 4 = 24$

E. 56; $56 \div 8 = 7$;
$56 \div 7 = 8$;
$7 \times 8 = 56$

F. 4; $4 \times 8 = 32$;
$32 \div 4 = 8$;
$8 \times 4 = 32$

 Cristina's News Station

TIMS Bit

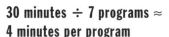

30 minutes ÷ 7 programs ≈ 4 minutes per program

Cristina's News Station has 7 programs every half hour: the international news, local news, weather, traffic, advertising, Joke of the Day, and Today's Music Single. If each program is the same length, approximately how many minutes long is each program?

60 Multiplying and Dividing with Zeros

A. $80 \times 400 =$ B. $2800 \div 70 =$

C. $7 \times 80,000 =$ D. $700 \times 6000 =$

E. $4800 \div 600 =$ F. $240 \div 4 =$

TIMS Bit

A. 32,000   B. 40

C. 560,000   D. 4,200,000

E. 8   F. 60

6P Number Sentences with 4, 6, 7, and 8

Use each number once in any order with any operation sign ($-$, $+$, $\times$, $\div$) to write number sentences. You can also use parentheses. Use these numbers: 4, 6, 7, 8.

(Remember, you must use each number once, but only once.)

A. _____ = 1

B. _____ = 10

C. _____ = 20

D. _____ = 200

TIMS Challenge

One example is provided for each.

A. $8 \div 4 - (7 - 6) = 1$

B. $4 \times 6 \div 8 + 7 = 10$

C. $8 \times 6 - 7 \times 4 = 20$

D. $(7 \times 8 - 6) \times 4 = 200$

6Q Quiz: The Last Six Facts

A. $6 \times 7 =$ B. $24 \div 6 =$

C. $8 \times 7 =$ D. $7 \times 4 =$

E. $48 \div 8 =$ F. $32 \div 4 =$

TIMS Bit

We recommend 1 minute for this quiz. Allow students to change pens after the time is up and complete the remaining problems in a different color. After students take the test, have them update their *Multiplication Facts I Know* and *Division Facts I Know* charts.

Unit 6 Home Practice

PART 1 *Triangle Flash Cards: Last Six Facts*

Study for the quiz on the multiplication and division facts for the last six facts
(4 × 6, 4 × 7, 4 × 8, 6 × 7, 6 × 8, and 7 × 8). Take home your *Triangle Flash
Cards: Last Six Facts* and your list of facts you need to study.

Ask a family member to choose one flash card at a time. To quiz you on a
multiplication fact, he or she should cover the corner containing the highest
number. Multiply the two uncovered numbers.

To quiz you on a division fact, your family member can cover one of the smaller
numbers. One of the smaller numbers is circled. The other has a square around it.
Use the two uncovered numbers to solve a division fact.

Ask your family member to mix up the multiplication and division facts. He or she
should sometimes cover the highest number, sometimes cover the circled number,
and sometimes cover the number in the square.

Your teacher will tell you when the quiz on the last six facts will be given.

Section 5

Facts Distribution

Multiplication and Division:
Review All Fact Groups • Weeks 19–25

Weeks 19–25

Math Facts Groups	Weeks	Daily Practice and Problems	Home Practice	Triangle Flash Cards	Facts Quizzes and Tests
Multiplication and Division: Review All Fact Groups	19–25	Unit 7: items 7C, 7G, 7K, 7O, 7S & 7W Unit 8: items 8B, 8C, 8I, 8K, 8M & 8Q	Unit 7 Part 1 Unit 8 Part 1	*Triangle Flash Cards: 5s, 10s, 2s, 3s, Square Numbers, 9s,* and the *Last Six Facts*	DPP item 8Q is an inventory test on all five groups of multiplication and division facts. The *Multiplication* and *Division Facts I Know* charts are updated.

Students may solve the items individually, in groups, or as a class. The items may also be assigned for homework. The DPPs are also available on the Teacher Resource CD.

Student Questions	Teacher Notes

7C Reviewing the Facts

Solve the given fact. Then name the other related fact or facts in the same fact family.

A. $5 \times 6 =$

B. $7 \times 4 =$

C. $24 \div 8 =$

D. $4 \times 10 =$

E. $81 \div 9 =$

F. $14 \div 7 =$

TIMS Task

In the next unit, you will test students on all five groups of facts—the 2s and 3s, 5s and 10s, 9s, square numbers, and the last six facts (4×6, 4×7, 4×8, 6×7, 6×8, and 7×8).

A. 30; $6 \times 5 = 30$;
   $30 \div 5 = 6$;
   $30 \div 6 = 5$

B. 28; $4 \times 7 = 28$;
   $28 \div 4 = 7$;
   $28 \div 7 = 4$

C. 3; $24 \div 3 = 8$;
   $8 \times 3 = 24$;
   $3 \times 8 = 24$

D. 40; $10 \times 4 = 40$;
   $40 \div 4 = 10$;
   $40 \div 10 = 4$

E. 9; $9 \times 9 = 81$

F. 2; $14 \div 2 = 7$;
   $7 \times 2 = 14$;
   $2 \times 7 = 14$

At some point during this unit, have student pairs review all the multiplication and division facts using the *Triangle Flash Cards*. Ask them to sort the cards into three piles: those facts they know and can answer quickly, those they can figure out with a strategy, and those they need to learn. Have students update their *Multiplication and Division Facts I Know* charts.

Reviewing the Facts

Solve the given fact. Then name the other related fact or facts in the same fact family.

A. $8 \times 6 =$

B. $12 \div 4 =$

C. $80 \div 8 =$

D. $40 \div 8 =$

E. $7 \times 9 =$

F. $2 \times 4 =$

TIMS Bit

A. 48; $6 \times 8 = 48$;
   $48 \div 6 = 8$;
   $48 \div 8 = 6$

B. 3; $12 \div 3 = 4$;
   $3 \times 4 = 12$;
   $4 \times 3 = 12$

C. 10; $80 \div 10 = 8$;
   $10 \times 8 = 80$;
   $8 \times 10 = 80$

D. 5; $40 \div 5 = 8$;
   $5 \times 8 = 40$;
   $8 \times 5 = 40$

E. 63; $9 \times 7 = 63$;
   $63 \div 7 = 9$;
   $63 \div 9 = 7$

F. 8; $4 \times 2 = 8$;
   $8 \div 2 = 4$;
   $8 \div 4 = 2$

7K Reviewing the Facts

Solve the given fact. Then name the other related fact or facts in the same fact family.

A. $10 \times 6 =$

B. $56 \div 7 =$

C. $45 \div 5 =$

D. $6 \times 2 =$

E. $18 \div 3 =$

F. $8 \times 4 =$

TIMS Bit

A. 60; $6 \times 10 = 60$;
    $60 \div 10 = 6$;
    $60 \div 6 = 10$

B. 8; $56 \div 8 = 7$;
    $7 \times 8 = 56$;
    $8 \times 7 = 56$

C. 9; $45 \div 9 = 5$;
    $5 \times 9 = 45$;
    $9 \times 5 = 45$

D. 12; $2 \times 6 = 12$;
    $12 \div 6 = 2$;
    $12 \div 2 = 6$

E. 6; $18 \div 6 = 3$;
    $6 \times 3 = 18$;
    $3 \times 6 = 18$

F. 32; $4 \times 8 = 32$;
    $32 \div 4 = 8$;
    $32 \div 8 = 4$

Have students update their *Multiplication* and *Division Facts I Know* charts. Remind students to take home their *Triangle Flash Cards* to review the facts they have yet to circle on their charts. The Home Practice for this unit reminds students to take home their flash cards.

Student Questions	Teacher Notes

 70 **Reviewing the Facts**

Solve the given fact. Then name the other related fact or facts in the same fact family.

A. $24 \div 4 =$

B. $5 \times 5 =$

C. $70 \div 10 =$

D. $18 \div 9 =$

E. $7 \times 6 =$

F. $15 \div 3 =$

TIMS Bit

A. 6; $24 \div 6 = 4$;
$6 \times 4 = 24$;
$4 \times 6 = 24$

B. 25; $25 \div 5 = 5$

C. 7; $70 \div 7 = 10$;
$10 \times 7 = 70$;
$7 \times 10 = 70$

D. 2; $18 \div 2 = 9$;
$2 \times 9 = 18$;
$9 \times 2 = 18$

E. 42; $6 \times 7 = 42$;
$42 \div 6 = 7$;
$42 \div 7 = 6$

F. 5; $15 \div 5 = 3$;
$5 \times 3 = 15$;
$3 \times 5 = 15$

7S **Reviewing the Facts**

Solve the given fact. Then name the other related fact or facts in the same fact family.

A. $6 \div 3 =$

B. $8 \times 8 =$

C. $35 \div 7 =$

D. $20 \div 5 =$

E. $9 \times 6 =$

F. $27 \div 9 =$

TIMS Bit

A. 2; $6 \div 2 = 3$;
$2 \times 3 = 6$;
$3 \times 2 = 6$

B. 64; $64 \div 8 = 8$

C. 5; $35 \div 5 = 7$;
$5 \times 7 = 35$;
$7 \times 5 = 35$

D. 4; $20 \div 4 = 5$;
$5 \times 4 = 20$;
$4 \times 5 = 20$

E. 54; $6 \times 9 = 54$;
$54 \div 6 = 9$;
$54 \div 9 = 6$

F. 3; $27 \div 3 = 9$;
$9 \times 3 = 27$;
$3 \times 9 = 27$

Reviewing the Facts

Solve the given fact. Then name the other related fact or facts in the same fact family.

A. $7 \times 3 =$

B. $36 \div 6 =$

C. $72 \div 8 =$

D. $4 \times 9 =$

E. $50 \div 5 =$

F. $7 \times 7 =$

TIMS Bit

$\boxed{\begin{smallmatrix}5\\ \times 7\end{smallmatrix}}$

A. 21; $3 \times 7 = 21$;
$21 \div 3 = 7$;
$21 \div 7 = 3$

B. 6; $6 \times 6 = 36$

C. 9; $72 \div 9 = 8$;
$8 \times 9 = 72$;
$9 \times 8 = 72$

D. 36; $9 \times 4 = 36$;
$36 \div 4 = 9$;
$36 \div 9 = 4$

E. 10; $50 \div 10 = 5$;
$10 \times 5 = 50$;
$5 \times 10 = 50$

F. 49; $49 \div 7 = 7$

Name _____ Date _____

Unit 7 **Home Practice**

PART 1 *Triangle Flash Cards: All the Facts*

Look at your *Multiplication* and *Division Facts I Know* charts. Take home your *Triangle Flash Cards* for all the facts you have not circled. With the help of a family member, use the cards to study a small group of facts (8 to 10 facts) each night.

Ask a family member to choose one flash card at a time. To quiz you on a multiplication fact, he or she should cover the corner containing the highest number. Multiply the two uncovered numbers.

To quiz you on a division fact, your family member can cover one of the smaller numbers. (One of the smaller numbers is circled. The other has a square around it.) Use the two uncovered numbers to solve a division fact.

Ask your family member to mix up the multiplication and division facts. He or she should sometimes cover the highest number, sometimes cover the circled number, and sometimes cover the number in the square.

Students may solve the items individually, in groups, or as a class. The items may also be assigned for homework. The DPPs are also available on the Teacher Resource CD.

Student Questions	Teacher Notes

 Multiplication and Division Facts

With a partner, use the *Triangle Flash Cards* to quiz each other on the multiplication facts. Have your partner cover the shaded number (the product). Use the two uncovered numbers to solve a multiplication fact. As you are quizzed, sort the cards into three piles: those facts you know well and can answer quickly, those you know using a strategy, and those you need to learn. Then, circle the facts you know well and can answer quickly on a clean copy of the *Multiplication Facts I Know* chart.

Next, quiz each other on the division facts. To quiz you on the division facts, have your partner cover the numbers in the circles first and then the numbers in the squares. Solve a division fact with the two uncovered numbers. Sort the cards and record your progress on a clean copy of the *Division Facts I Know* chart.

List the facts you have not yet circled on both your charts. Take the flash cards for these facts home so you can practice them. Your teacher will tell you when to expect the test on these facts.

TIMS Task

Students can take home the flash cards for the facts they need to practice, or they can make cards for those facts on copies of the *Triangle Flash Card Master*, which follows the Home Practice in the *Discovery Assignment Book*. Part 1 of the Home Practice reminds students to take home these newly prepared flash cards to study for the test.

The *Multiplication Facts I Know* and *Division Facts I Know* charts were distributed in the *Unit Resource Guide* for Unit 2 Lesson 2. See this Lesson Guide for more information.

Inform students when you will give the test on these facts. This test assesses students on multiplication and division facts. It is DPP item 8Q. A blackline master of the test immediately follows the DPP.

All the *Triangle Flash Cards*, *Triangle Flash Card Master*, *Facts I Know* charts, and *Multiplication and Division Fact Inventory Test* are in the *Grade 5 Facts Resource Guide*.

Fact Practice I

Find *n* to make each number sentence true.

A. $5 \times 8 = n$ B. $3 \times n = 21$

C. $36 \div 6 = n$ D. $n \times 5 = 10$

E. $10 \times 4 = n$ F. $20 \div n = 4$

G. $12 \div 3 = n$ H. $9 \times 6 = n$

I. $n \times 8 = 64$

TIMS Bit

A. 40   B. 7
C. 6   D. 2
E. 40   F. 5
G. 4   H. 54
I. 8

8I **Fact Practice II**

Find *n* to make each number sentence true.

A. $10 \times n = 90$ B. $16 \div 2 = n$

C. $3 \times 5 = n$ D. $28 \div 4 = n$

E. $4 \times n = 36$ F. $50 \div n = 10$

G. $6 \times 2 = n$ H. $24 \div 3 = n$

I. $7 \times n = 63$

TIMS Bit

A. 9   B. 8
C. 15   D. 7
E. 9   F. 5
G. 12   H. 8
I. 9

8K **Fact Practice III**

Find *n* to make each number sentence true.

A. $70 \times 6 = n$ B. $90 \times 90 = n$

C. $3000 \div 6 = n$ D. $14{,}000 \div 200 = n$

E. $40 \times 400 = n$ F. $56{,}000 \div 80 = n$

G. $30 \times n = 180$ H. $5000 \times 9 = n$

I. $800 \div 10 = n$

TIMS Bit

A. 420   B. 8100
C. 500   D. 70
E. 16,000   F. 700
G. 6   H. 45,000
I. 80

Fact Practice IV

Find *n* to make each number sentence true.
Then name one other fact in the same
fact family.

A. $9 \times 2 = n$ B. $30 \div 5 = n$

C. $7 \times 7 = n$ D. $32 \div 8 = n$

E. $10 \times 7 = n$ F. $6 \times 8 = n$

G. $27 \div 3 = n$ H. $8 \times 9 = n$

I. $24 \div 4 = n$

A. 18; $2 \times 9 = 18$;
   $18 \div 2 = 9$;
   $18 \div 9 = 2$

B. 6; $30 \div 6 = 5$;
   $6 \times 5 = 30$;
   $5 \times 6 = 30$

C. 49; $49 \div 7 = 7$

D. 4; $32 \div 4 = 8$;
   $4 \times 8 = 32$;
   $8 \times 4 = 32$

E. 70; $7 \times 10 = 70$;
   $70 \div 10 = 7$;
   $70 \div 7 = 10$

F. 48; $8 \times 6 = 48$;
   $48 \div 8 = 6$;
   $48 \div 6 = 8$

G. 9; $27 \div 9 = 3$;
   $9 \times 3 = 27$;
   $3 \times 9 = 27$

H. 72; $9 \times 8 = 72$;
   $72 \div 8 = 9$;
   $72 \div 9 = 8$

I. 6; $24 \div 6 = 4$;
   $6 \times 4 = 24$;
   $4 \times 6 = 24$

8Q *Multiplication and Division Fact Inventory Test*

Students take a test that contains the facts from all five groups of facts studied in Units 2–8—the 5s and 10s, 2s and 3s, square numbers, 9s, and the last six facts.

Students should have two pens or pencils of different colors. During the first four minutes, students write their answers using one color pen or pencil. Encourage students first to answer all the facts they know well and can answer quickly. Then they should go back and use strategies to solve the rest. After four minutes, give students more time to complete the remaining items with the other color pen or pencil.

Using the test results, students should update their new *Multiplication* and *Division Facts I Know* charts.

TIMS Bit

The test follows DPP item 8R. It lets you and your students see which multiplication and division facts they still need to study. We recommend 4 minutes for this test.

Students can continue to use the *Triangle Flash Cards* to practice the facts that are not yet circled. Students will continue to practice math facts in the DPP.

Students may include their tests in their portfolios.

Multiplication and Division Fact Inventory Test

You will need two pens or pencils of different colors. Use the first color when you begin the test. When your teacher tells you to switch pens, finish the test using the second color.

$5 \times 5 =$	$24 \div 6 =$	$10 \times 7 =$	$15 \div 3 =$
$8 \times 7 =$	$20 \div 10 =$	$7 \times 7 =$	$10 \times 3 =$
$28 \div 4 =$	$54 \div 9 =$	$36 \div 6 =$	$9 \times 5 =$
$5 \times 2 =$	$20 \div 5 =$	$8 \times 8 =$	$60 \div 6 =$
$4 \times 2 =$	$24 \div 8 =$	$2 \times 7 =$	$10 \times 10 =$
$10 \times 9 =$	$16 \div 4 =$	$9 \times 9 =$	$16 \div 2 =$
$8 \times 4 =$	$42 \div 7 =$	$9 \times 4 =$	$10 \times 5 =$
$3 \times 3 =$	$35 \div 7 =$	$7 \times 9 =$	$48 \div 6 =$
$6 \div 3 =$	$3 \times 6 =$	$27 \div 3 =$	$10 \times 4 =$
$72 \div 8 =$	$6 \times 5 =$	$12 \div 4 =$	$7 \times 3 =$
$18 \div 2 =$	$40 \div 8 =$	$2 \times 2 =$	$80 \div 8 =$
$12 \div 6 =$			

Name _____   Date _____

Unit 8   Home Practice

PART 1 *Triangle Flash Cards:* **All the Facts**

Study for the test on the multiplication and division facts. Take home the flash cards for the facts you need to study.

Ask a family member to choose one flash card at a time. To quiz you on a multiplication fact, he or she should cover the corner containing the highest number. Multiply the two uncovered numbers.

To quiz you on a division fact, your family member can cover one of the smaller numbers. One of the smaller numbers is circled. The other has a square around it. Use the two uncovered numbers to solve a division fact.

Ask your family member to mix up the multiplication and division facts. He or she should sometimes cover the highest number, sometimes cover the circled number, and sometimes cover the number in the square.

Your teacher will tell you when the test on the facts will be given.

Section 5

Facts Distribution

**Multiplication and Division: Review •
Weeks 26–39**

Math Facts Groups	Weeks	Daily Practice and Problems	Home Practice	Triangle Flash Cards	Facts Quizzes and Tests
Multiplication and Division: Review (without formal assessment) **Distribute these items over the remainder of the school year.**	26–39	Unit 9: items 9G, 9K, 9M, 9Q & 9S Unit 10: items 10A, 10E, 10I, 10K & 10O Unit 11: items 11E, 11I, 11M, 11P, 11Q, 11S & 11U Unit 12: items 12A, 12E, 12G, 12I, 12K & 12M Unit 13: items 13A, 13E, 13H, 13I, 13M, 13Q & 13S Unit 14: items 14E, 14G, 14K, 14O, 14P, 14S & 14W Unit 15: items 15E, 15F & 15I Unit 16: items 16E, 16G, 16I, 16O & 16S	Unit 12 Part 2 Unit 13 Part 1 Unit 15 Parts 1 & 2		

Unit ⑨ Daily Practice and Problems

Students may solve the items individually, in groups, or as a class. The items may also be assigned for homework. The DPPs are also available on the Teacher Resource CD.

Student Questions	Teacher Notes
9G Practicing the Facts	**TIMS Bit**

9G Practicing the Facts

A. $300 \div 50 =$

B. $400 \div 4 =$

C. $150 \div 3 =$

D. $100 \div 10 =$

E. $45 \div 5 =$

F. $2500 \div 5 =$

G. $600 \div 100 =$

H. $35 \div 7 =$

I. $10 \div 5 =$

TIMS Bit

A. 6
B. 100
C. 50
D. 10
E. 9
F. 500
G. 6
H. 5
I. 2

9K More Fact Practice

Find *n* to make each number sentence true.

A. $n \times 5 = 40$ B. $n \times 7 = 70$

C. $n \div 4 = 5$ D. $80 \div n = 10$

E. $10 \times n = 50$ F. $30 \div 5 = n$

G. $9 \times 10 = n$ H. $15 \div n = 5$

I. $n \times 8 = 80$

TIMS Bit

A. 8   B. 10
C. 20   D. 8
E. 5   F. 6
G. 90   H. 3
I. 10

Student Questions	Teacher Notes

9M **Multiplying and Dividing by Multiples of Ten**

A. $80 \times 500 =$

B. $60 \times 100 =$

C. $20 \times 5000 =$

D. $3000 \div 60 =$

E. $70,000 \div 100 =$

F. $4500 \div 90 =$

TIMS Bit

A. 40,000

B. 6000

C. 100,000

D. 50

E. 700

F. 50

9Q **Dividing by Multiples of Ten**

A. $9000 \div 100 =$

B. $45,000 \div 900 =$

C. $20,000 \div 2 =$

D. $350 \div 70 =$

E. $250,000 \div 500 =$

F. $30,000 \div 30 =$

TIMS Bit

A. 90

B. 50

C. 10,000

D. 5

E. 500

F. 1000

9S **Reviewing Division Facts: 5s and 10s**

A. $45 \div 5 =$

B. $25 \div 5 =$

C. $10 \div 2 =$

D. $60 \div 10 =$

E. $40 \div 8 =$

F. $30 \div 3 =$

G. $20 \div 5 =$

H. $80 \div 10 =$

I. $30 \div 6 =$

J. $35 \div 5 =$

K. $15 \div 3 =$

L. $50 \div 10 =$

M. $70 \div 10 =$

N. $90 \div 9 =$

O. $40 \div 4 =$

P. $20 \div 2 =$

Q. $100 \div 10 =$

TIMS Bit

A. 9

B. 5

C. 5

D. 6

E. 5

F. 10

G. 4

H. 8

I. 5

J. 7

K. 5

L. 5

M. 7

N. 10

O. 10

P. 10

Q. 10

Unit 10   Daily Practice and Problems

Students may solve the items individually, in groups, or as a class. The items may also be assigned for homework. The DPPs are also available on the Teacher Resource CD.

Student Questions	Teacher Notes

10A   Fact Practice

TIMS Task

Solve for n.

A. $9 \div n = 3$ B. $16 \div n = 8$

C. $6 \times n = 36$ D. $2 \times n = 12$

E. $n \div 10 = 10$ F. $n \div 8 = 8$

G. $n \times 5 = 25$ H. $n \times 9 = 81$

I. $7 \times 7 = n$ J. $2 \times 9 = n$

A. $n = 3$
B. $n = 2$
C. $n = 6$
D. $n = 6$
E. $n = 100$
F. $n = 64$
G. $n = 5$
H. $n = 9$
I. $n = 49$
J. $n = 18$

10E   Practicing the Facts

TIMS Bit

A. $20 \div 2 =$ B. $4 \div 2 =$

C. $14 \div 7 =$ D. $100 \div 10 =$

E. $10 \div 5 =$ F. $9 \div 3 =$

G. $6 \div 3 =$ H. $64 \div 8 =$

I. $18 \div 2 =$

A. 10   B. 2
C. 2   D. 10
E. 2   F. 3
G. 2   H. 8
I. 9

101 **Dividing by Multiples of Ten**

TIMS Bit

A. $2000 \div 100 =$

B. $16{,}000 \div 200 =$

C. $40{,}000 \div 2 =$

D. $160 \div 40 =$

E. $25{,}000 \div 50 =$

F. $80{,}000 \div 40 =$

G. $1400 \div 7 =$

H. $900 \div 3 =$

I. $8100 \div 900 =$

A. 20
B. 80
C. 20,000
D. 4
E. 500
F. 2000
G. 200
H. 300
I. 9

10K **Multiplying and Dividing by Multiples of Ten**

TIMS Bit

A. $80 \times 800 =$

B. $60 \times 200 =$

C. $90 \times 200 =$

D. $3600 \div 60 =$

E. $4900 \div 70 =$

F. $10{,}000 \div 50 =$

A. 64,000
B. 12,000
C. 18,000
D. 60
E. 70
F. 200

100 Practice: 2s and Squares

A. $10 \div 5 =$ B. $25 \div 5 =$

C. $20 \div 2 =$ D. $6 \div 3 =$

E. $4 \div 2 =$ F. $9 \div 3 =$

G. $36 \div 6 =$ H. $8 \div 2 =$

I. $100 \div 10 =$ J. $12 \div 2 =$

K. $64 \div 8 =$ L. $14 \div 7 =$

M. $16 \div 2 =$ N. $49 \div 7 =$

O. $16 \div 4 =$ P. $18 \div 9 =$

Q. $81 \div 9 =$

TIMS Bit

A. 2   B. 5
C. 10   D. 2
E. 2   F. 3
G. 6   H. 4
I. 10   J. 6
K. 8   L. 2
M. 8   N. 7
O. 4   P. 2
Q. 9

Unit 11   Daily Practice and Problems

Students may solve the items individually, in groups, or as a class. The items may also be assigned for homework. The DPPs are also available on the Teacher Resource CD.

Student Questions	Teacher Notes

11E   Division Practice I

A. $72 \div 9 =$ B. $24 \div 3 =$

C. $45 \div 9 =$ D. $15 \div 3 =$

E. $36 \div 9 =$ F. $12 \div 3 =$

TIMS Bit

A. 8   B. 8

C. 5   D. 5

E. 4   F. 4

11I   Division Practice II

A. $810 \div 90 =$ B. $300 \div 30 =$

C. $6300 \div 70 =$ D. $180 \div 20 =$

E. $2100 \div 70 =$ F. $6000 \div 20 =$

G. $900 \div 30 =$ H. $900 \div 10 =$

I. $540 \div 90 =$

TIMS Bit

A. 9   B. 10

C. 90   D. 9

E. 30   F. 300

G. 30   H. 90

I. 6

11M   Division Practice III

A. $180 \div 6 =$

B. $270 \div 3 =$

C. $4500 \div 50 =$

D. $2400 \div 800 =$

E. $36,000 \div 40 =$

F. $90,000 \div 100 =$

TIMS Bit

A. 30

B. 90

C. 90

D. 3

E. 900

F. 900

11P Finding Factors

1. Find all the factors for the following numbers. Tell which numbers are prime.

   A. 23

   B. 258

   C. 39

   D. 73

   E. 1278

2. Draw a factor tree for each composite number above. Then write its prime factorization.

TIMS Task

1. A. 1, 23; prime

   B. 1, 2, 3, 6, 43, 86, 129, 258

   C. 1, 3, 13, 39

   D. 1, 73; prime

   E. 1, 2, 3, 6, 9, 18, 71, 142, 213, 426, 639, 1278

2. A. prime

   B. $2 \times 3 \times 43$

   C. 3×13

   D. prime

   E. $2 \times 3^2 \times 71$

11Q Division Fact Practice IV

A. $630 \div n = 7$

B. $n \div 300 = 7$

C. $5400 \div n = 90$

D. $27{,}000 \div 30 = n$

E. $8100 \div 900 = n$

F. $1800 \div n = 600$

TIMS Bit

A. 90

B. 2100

C. 60

D. 900

E. 9

F. 3

Student Questions	Teacher Notes

11S   Practice: 3s and 9s

A. $30 \div 3 =$ B. $45 \div 5 =$

C. $90 \div 10 =$ D. $18 \div 6 =$

E. $24 \div 8 =$ F. $9 \div 3 =$

G. $54 \div 6 =$ H. $18 \div 2 =$

I. $81 \div 9 =$ J. $12 \div 3 =$

K. $63 \div 7 =$ L. $21 \div 7 =$

M. $15 \div 5 =$ N. $6 \div 3 =$

O. $27 \div 9 =$ P. $36 \div 4 =$

Q. $72 \div 8 =$

TIMS Bit

A. 10	B. 9
C. 9	D. 3
E. 3	F. 3
G. 9	H. 9
I. 9	J. 4
K. 9	L. 3
M. 3	N. 2
O. 3	P. 9
Q. 9	

11U   Products of Prime

Solve the following in your head.

A. $2^2 \times 3^2 =$

B. $5^2 \times 2^2 =$

C. $2^3 \times 3 =$

D. $3^2 \times 7 =$

TIMS Bit

A. 36	B. 100
C. 24	D. 63

Unit 12 Daily Practice and Problems

Students may solve the items individually, in groups, or as a class. The items may also be assigned for homework. The DPPs are also available on the Teacher Resource CD.

Student Questions	Teacher Notes

12A Practice: Last Six Facts

A. $48 \div 6 =$ B. $56 \div 8 =$

C. $24 \div 4 =$ D. $32 \div 8 =$

E. $42 \div 6 =$ F. $28 \div 7 =$

TIMS Bit

A. 8   B. 7

C. 6   D. 4

E. 7   F. 4

12E Division Facts

A. $240 \div 40 =$

B. $4800 \div 60 =$

C. $2800 \div 700 =$

D. $560 \div 70 =$

E. $42{,}000 \div 600 =$

F. $3200 \div 80 =$

TIMS Bit

A. 6

B. 80

C. 4

D. 8

E. 70

F. 40

12G Division Facts

Find the number n that makes each sentence true.

A. $42 \div 7 = n$ B. $320 \div 4 = n$

C. $56 \div n = 7$ D. $28 \div n = 7$

E. $n \div 6 = 4$ F. $n \div 8 = 6$

TIMS Bit

A. 6   B. 80

C. 8   D. 4

E. 24   F. 48

Student Questions	Teacher Notes

12I **More Division Fact Practice**

Find the number *n* that makes each sentence true.

A. $56 \div n = 8$

B. $480 \div n = 60$

C. $n \times 400 = 24{,}000$

D. $80 \times n = 3200$

E. $60 \times n = 420$

F. $n \div 7 = 400$

TIMS Bit

A. 7

B. 8

C. 60

D. 40

E. 7

F. 2800

12K **Division**

Try to solve the following problems in your head. Write the quotients as mixed numbers. Fractions should be in lowest terms.

A. $30 \div 7 =$ B. $60 \div 8 =$

C. $47 \div 6 =$ D. $26 \div 6 =$

E. $51 \div 6 =$ F. $35 \div 4 =$

TIMS Bit

A. $4\frac{2}{7}$ B. $7\frac{1}{2}$

C. $7\frac{5}{6}$ D. $4\frac{1}{3}$

E. $8\frac{1}{2}$ F. $8\frac{3}{4}$

12M **Fact Practice**

A. $60 \times 80 =$

B. $420 \div 70 =$

C. $32{,}000 \div 400 =$

D. $70 \times 8 =$

E. $2400 \div 6 =$

F. $7000 \times 40 =$

TIMS Bit

A. 4800

B. 6

C. 80

D. 560

E. 400

F. 280,000

Unit 12 Home Practice

PART 2 Division Practice

1. Solve the following problems in your head or with paper and pencil. Write the quotient as a mixed number. Reduce all fractions to lowest terms.

   A. $33 \div 4 =$ **B.** $76 \div 9 =$ **C.** $17 \div 2 =$

   D. $108 \div 10 =$ **E.** $54 \div 7 =$ **F.** $41 \div 6 =$

   G. $42 \div 8 =$ **H.** $23 \div 6 =$ **I.** $67 \div 8 =$

2. Use a calculator to find the answers to the following. Write your answers as mixed numbers. Reduce all fractions to lowest terms.

   A. $1388 \div 16 =$ **B.** $18{,}478 \div 24 =$ **C.** $43{,}956 \div 32 =$

Unit 13 Daily Practice and Problems

Students may solve the items individually, in groups, or as a class. The items may also be assigned for homework. The DPPs are also available on the Teacher Resource CD.

Student Questions	Teacher Notes

13A How Square Can You Be?

Try to do the following in your head.

A. $6^2 \div 4 =$

B. $9^2 \div 9 =$

C. $4^2 \div 8 =$

D. $4^2 \div 2^2 =$

E. $10^2 \div 5^2 =$

F. $8^2 \div 4^2 =$

TIMS Bit

A. 9   B. 9

C. 2   D. 4

E. 4   F. 4

13E Practicing the Facts

A. $200 \div 40 =$

B. $640 \div 80 =$

C. $400 \div 10 =$

D. $1200 \div 60 =$

E. $900 \div 90 =$

F. $490 \div 70 =$

G. $8000 \div 40 =$

H. $40{,}000 \div 80 =$

I. $1800 \div 20 =$

J. $400 \div 20 =$

TIMS Bit

A. 5

B. 8

C. 40

D. 20

E. 10

F. 7

G. 200

H. 500

I. 90

J. 20

Student Questions	Teacher Notes

13H Remainders

Solve the following problems. Write the quotients first as whole numbers with remainders, then as mixed numbers, and finally as decimals.

A. $42 \div 5 =$

B. $19 \div 5 =$

C. $7 \div 5 =$

TIMS Task

A. 8 R2, $8\frac{2}{5}$, 8.4

B. 3 R4, $3\frac{4}{5}$, 3.8

C. 1 R2, $1\frac{2}{5}$, 1.4

Students should have calculators available.

13I More Facts

Find the value of n that makes these number sentences true.

A. $80 \div 10 = n$

B. $n \div 8 = 2$

C. $30 \div n = 5$

D. $16 \div n = 4$

E. $n \div 9 = 5$

F. $100 \div 10 = n$

G. $100 \div 5 = n$

H. $n \div 3 = 10$

I. $60 \div 2 = n$

J. $9 \div n = 3$

TIMS Bit

A. 8

B. 16

C. 6

D. 4

E. 45

F. 10

G. 20

H. 30

I. 30

J. 3

13M Facts

Find the value of n that makes these number sentences true.

A. $50 \div 5 = n$

B. $n \div 3 = 5$

C. $36 \div n = 6$

D. $40 \div 20 = n$

E. $700 \div 10 = n$

F. $n \div 5 = 5$

G. $81 \div n = 9$

H. $200 \div 2 = n$

I. $n \div 7 = 2$

J. $35 \div n = 5$

TIMS Bit

A. 10

B. 15

C. 6

D. 2

E. 70

F. 25

G. 9

H. 100

I. 14

J. 7

13Q Using the Facts

Try to solve the following in your head.

A. $102 \div 10 =$

B. $13 \div 2 =$

C. $39 \div 5 =$

D. $37 \div 6 =$

E. $84 \div 9 =$

F. $63 \div 6 =$

TIMS Bit

A. 10 R2

B. 6 R1

C. 7 R4

D. 6 R1

E. 9 R3

F. 10 R3

13S Division Fact Practice

A. $16 \div 8 =$

B. $35 \div 7 =$

C. $49 \div 7 =$

D. $40 \div 10 =$

E. $15 \div 5 =$

F. $16 \div 4 =$

G. $50 \div 5 =$

H. $18 \div 2 =$

I. $70 \div 7 =$

J. $20 \div 10 =$

K. $81 \div 9 =$

L. $64 \div 8 =$

M. $6 \div 2 =$

N. $30 \div 5 =$

O. $100 \div 10 =$

A. 2   B. 5
C. 7   D. 4
E. 3   F. 4
G. 10   H. 9
I. 10   J. 2
K. 9   L. 8
M. 3   N. 6
O. 10

Unit 13 Home Practice

PART 1 Division Practice

A. 45 ÷ 9 =

B. 4 ÷ 2 =

C. 10 ÷ 5 =

D. 9 ÷ 3 =

E. 60 ÷ 6 =

F. 25 ÷ 5 =

G. 40 ÷ 5 =

H. 36 ÷ 6 =

I. 30 ÷ 10 =

J. 8 ÷ 4 =

K. 20 ÷ 4 =

L. 12 ÷ 6 =

M. 80 ÷ 8 =

N. 14 ÷ 2 =

O. 90 ÷ 10 =

Unit 14 Daily Practice and Problems

Students may solve the items individually, in groups, or as a class. The items may also be assigned for homework. The DPPs are also available on the Teacher Resource CD.

Student Questions	Teacher Notes

14E Division Fact Practice

A. $21 \div 7 =$

B. $63 \div 9 =$

C. $48 \div 8 =$

D. $12 \div 4 =$

E. $32 \div 4 =$

F. $30 \div 10 =$

G. $45 \div 5 =$

H. $18 \div 9 =$

TIMS Bit

A. 3   B. 7

C. 6   D. 3

E. 8   F. 3

G. 9   H. 2

14G Division Fact Practice

A. $560 \div 80 =$

B. $180 \div 30 =$

C. $280 \div 70 =$

D. $7200 \div 80 =$

E. $6000 \div 300 =$

F. $240 \div 80 =$

G. $360 \div 40 =$

H. $900 \div 30 =$

TIMS Bit

A. 7   B. 6

C. 4   D. 90

E. 20   F. 3

G. 9   H. 30

14K Division Fact Practice

A. $81 \div 9 = n$

B. $42 \div n = 7$

C. $n \div 3 = 9$

D. $n \div 6 = 4$

E. $15 \div n = 3$

F. $54 \div 6 = n$

TIMS Bit

A. 9   B. 6

C. 27   D. 24

E. 5   F. 9

---

140 Division

A. $3200 \div 80 =$

B. $63{,}000 \div 70 =$

C. $210 \div 3 =$

D. $480 \div 60 =$

E. $5400 \div 900 =$

F. $2400 \div 4 =$

TIMS Bit

A. 40

B. 900

C. 70

D. 8

E. 6

F. 600

14P Prime Factors

Write each of the following numbers as a product of primes using exponents. Use factor trees to organize your work.

A. 3600

B. 2800

C. 4500

TIMS Bit

Have students share their strategies. One way to start the factor trees is to think of the facts. 3600 = 60 × 60 or 40 × 90. Likewise, 2800 = 40 × 70 and 4500 = 90 × 50. Another way is to factor out 100 first and begin with 36 × 100, 28 × 100, and 45 × 100.

A. $2^4 \times 3^2 \times 5^2$

B. $2^4 \times 5^2 \times 7$

C. $2^2 \times 5^3 \times 3^2$

Division

Solve the following using mental math.

A. 30 ÷ 8 =

B. 40 ÷ 9 =

C. 45 ÷ 6 =

D. 15 ÷ 4 =

E. 34 ÷ 7 =

F. 62 ÷ 8 =

TIMS Bit

A. 3 R6

B. 4 R4

C. 7 R3

D. 3 R3

E. 4 R6

F. 7 R6

Division Fact Practice

A. 48 ÷ 8 =

B. 6 ÷ 2 =

C. 72 ÷ 9 =

D. 32 ÷ 4 =

E. 54 ÷ 9 =

F. 90 ÷ 9 =

G. 30 ÷ 3 =

H. 45 ÷ 9 =

I. 28 ÷ 4 =

J. 18 ÷ 3 =

K. 24 ÷ 3 =

L. 9 ÷ 3 =

M. 42 ÷ 7 =

N. 18 ÷ 9 =

O. 81 ÷ 9 =

P. 12 ÷ 4 =

Q. 63 ÷ 9 =

R. 21 ÷ 3 =

S. 15 ÷ 3 =

T. 56 ÷ 7 =

U. 27 ÷ 3 =

V. 36 ÷ 9 =

W. 24 ÷ 6 =

A. 6
B. 3
C. 8
D. 8
E. 6
F. 10
G. 10
H. 5
I. 7
J. 6
K. 8
L. 3
M. 6
N. 2
O. 9
P. 3
Q. 7
R. 7
S. 5
T. 8
U. 9
V. 4
W. 4

Unit 15 · Daily Practice and Problems

Students may solve the items individually, in groups, or as a class. The items may also be assigned for homework. The DPPs are also available on the Teacher Resource CD.

Student Questions	Teacher Notes

15E Division Fact Practice

A. $42 \div 7 =$

B. $10 \div 5 =$

C. $9 \div 3 =$

D. $100 \div 10 =$

E. $40 \div 8 =$

F. $16 \div 2 =$

G. $21 \div 7 =$

H. $72 \div 9 =$

I. $27 \div 3 =$

J. $49 \div 7 =$

K. $20 \div 4 =$

L. $40 \div 4 =$

TIMS Bit

A. 6   B. 2
C. 3   D. 10
E. 5   F. 8
G. 3   H. 8
I. 9   J. 7
K. 5   L. 10

15F Order of Operations

Solve the following problems using mental math or paper and pencil.

A. $(12 - 2 \times 4) \div 4 =$

B. $4 + 6 \times 5 \div 3 =$

C. $45 \div 9 - 15 \div 5 =$

D. $4 \times 6 + 0 \times 5 =$

E. $40 \div (5 + 3) \times 7 =$

F. $7^2 - 3^2 =$

G. $4^2 \times 2 =$

TIMS Bit

A. 1
B. 14
C. 2
D. 24
E. 35
F. 40
G. 32

151 **Division Fact Practice**

A. $60 \div 10 = n$ B. $63 \div 7 = n$

C. $81 \div n = 9$ D. $18 \div n = 6$

E. $n \div 2 = 6$ F. $n \div 5 = 9$

G. $36 \div 9 = n$ H. $16 \div n = 4$

I. $n \div 3 = 10$ J. $30 \div 6 = n$

K. $18 \div 9 = n$ L. $36 \div n = 6$

TIMS Bit

$\boxed{\begin{array}{r} 5 \\ \times\, 7 \end{array}}$

A. 6   B. 9

C. 9   D. 3

E. 12   F. 45

G. 4   H. 4

I. 30   J. 5

K. 2   L. 6

Unit 15 Home Practice

PART 1 Division Facts

Solve the following problems.

A. $480 \div 60 =$

B. $400 \div 20 =$

C. $800 \div 10 =$

D. $5600 \div 70 =$

E. $2800 \div 40 =$

F. $2400 \div 30 =$

G. $800 \div 40 =$

H. $900 \div 90 =$

I. $1200 \div 40 =$

J. $500 \div 10 =$

PART 2 Number Sense

Solve the following problems in your head.

I. Find the number N that makes each sentence true.

A. $30 \div N = 6$ B. $N \div 6 = 7$ C. $24 \div 6 = N$ D. $36 \div N = 9$

E. $N \div 8 = 8$ F. $16 \div N = 2$ G. $21 \div 3 = N$ H. $32 \div N = 8$

2. Solve.

A. $40{,}000 \div 80 =$ B. $720 \div 90 =$ C. $3600 \div 6 =$ D. $270 \div 30 =$

E. $48{,}000 \div 80 =$ F. $2000 \div 5 =$ G. $81{,}000 \div 90 =$ H. $3500 \div 70 =$

3. Follow the order of operations to solve each of the following.

A. $5 \times 3 + 14 =$ B. $(33 + 7) \times 9 =$ C. $45 + 45 \div 9 =$ D. $7^2 + 8 \times 3 =$

Unit 16 · Daily Practice and Problems

Students may solve the items individually, in groups, or as a class. The items may also be assigned for homework. The DPPs are also available on the Teacher Resource CD.

Student Questions	Teacher Notes

16E Division Fact Practice

A. $50 \div 5 =$ B. $12 \div 3 =$

C. $90 \div 10 =$ D. $8 \div 2 =$

E. $24 \div 8 =$ F. $28 \div 7 =$

G. $56 \div 8 =$ H. $80 \div 8 =$

I. $4 \div 2 =$ J. $48 \div 8 =$

TIMS Bit

A. 10   B. 4

C. 9   D. 4

E. 3   F. 4

G. 7   H. 10

I. 2   J. 6

16G Division Fact Practice

A. $40 \div 10 = n$ B. $n \div 5 = 4$

C. $49 \div n = 7$ D. $27 \div n = 3$

E. $72 \div n = 9$ F. $21 \div 3 = n$

G. $n \div 8 = 2$ H. $n \div 5 = 8$

I. $100 \div 10 = n$ J. $9 \div 3 = n$

K. $n \div 2 = 5$ L. $42 \div n = 7$

TIMS Bit

A. 4   B. 20

C. 7   D. 9

E. 8   F. 7

G. 16   H. 40

I. 10   J. 3

K. 10   L. 6

Student Questions	**Teacher Notes**

161 **Division Fact Practice**

A. $36 \div 6 =$

B. $180 \div 20 =$

C. $300 \div 50 =$

D. $3000 \div 100 =$

E. $160 \div 40 =$

F. $36,000 \div 400 =$

G. $450 \div 90 =$

H. $1200 \div 60 =$

I. $18,000 \div 600 =$

J. $81,000 \div 90 =$

K. $630 \div 90 =$

L. $60,000 \div 6 =$

TIMS Bit

A. 6
B. 9
C. 6
D. 30
E. 4
F. 90
G. 5
H. 20
I. 30
J. 900
K. 7
L. 10,000

---

160 **Division Fact Practice**

A. $6 \div 3 = n$ B. $25 \div 5 = n$

C. $n \div 3 = 9$ D. $20 \div n = 10$

E. $24 \div n = 4$ F. $n \div 8 = 8$

G. $54 \div 9 = n$ H. $15 \div 5 = n$

I. $n \div 4 = 8$ J. $n \div 10 = 7$

K. $14 \div n = 2$ L. $35 \div n = 7$

TIMS Bit

A. 2   B. 5
C. 27   D. 2
E. 6   F. 64
G. 6   H. 3
I. 32   J. 70
K. 7   L. 5

Mental Math

Use mental math and patterns to complete the following table. Tell the rule for the table.

Input	Output
0	1
1	6
2	11
	21
7	
11	
	26

TIMS Bit

$n \times 5 + 1$

Input	Output
0	1
1	6
2	11
4	21
7	36
11	56
5	26

Math Facts Games

This section contains games and activities that can be used by those students who need extra practice with the multiplication and division facts. Some of the games and activities are from previous grades of the *Math Trailblazers* curriculum.

Floor Tiler

Players

This is a game for two to four players.

Materials

- $\frac{1}{2}$ sheet of *Centimeter Grid Paper* per player
- *Spinner 1–4*
- *Spinner 1–10*
- a crayon or marker for each player

Rules

1. The first player makes two spins so that he or she has two numbers. The player may either spin one spinner twice or spin each spinner once.

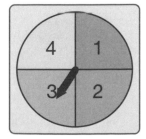 

2. The player must then find the **product** of the two numbers he or she spun. For example, $3 \times 4 = $ **12**.

3. After finding the product, the player colors in a rectangle that has the same number of grid squares on the grid paper. For example, he or she might color in 3 rows of 4 squares for a total of 12 squares. But the player could have colored in 2 rows of 6 squares or 1 row of 12 squares instead. (Remember, the squares colored in must connect so that they form a rectangle.)

4. Once the player has made his or her rectangle, the player draws an outline around it and writes its number sentence inside. For example, a player who colored in 3 rows of 4 squares would write "$3 \times 4 = 12$." A player who colored in 2 rows of 6 squares would write "$2 \times 6 = 12$."

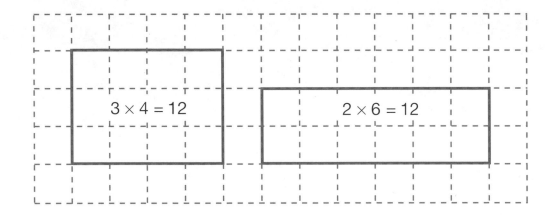

5. Players take turns spinning and filling in their grids.

6. If a player is unable to fill in a rectangle for his or her spin, he or she loses the turn, and the next player can play.

7. The first player to fill in his or her grid paper completely wins the game.

8. If no player is able to color in a rectangle in three rounds of spinning, the player with the fewest squares of the grid left is the winner.

Centimeter Grid Paper

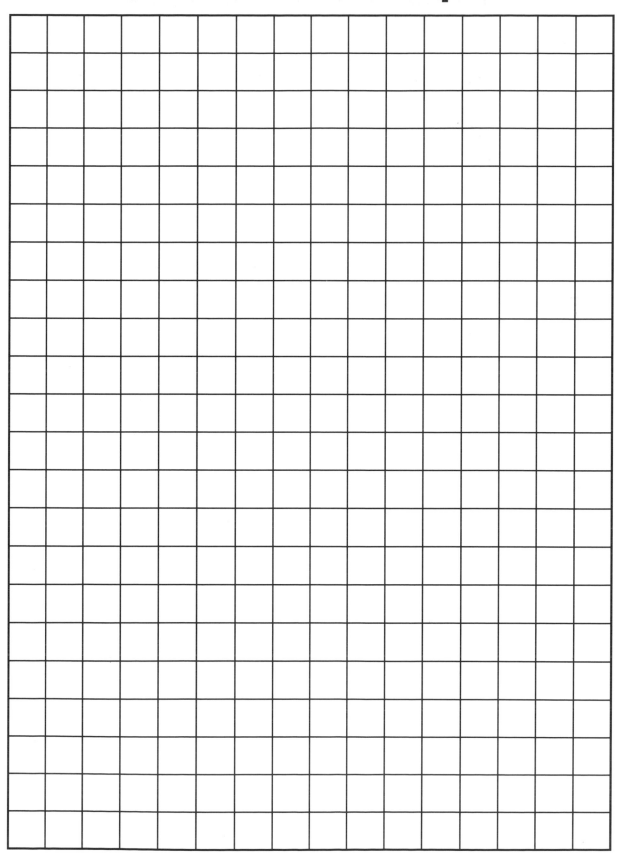

Spinners 1-4 and 1-10

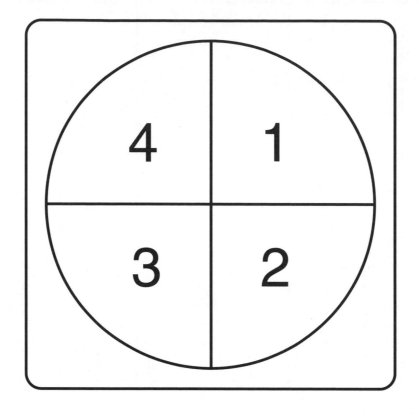

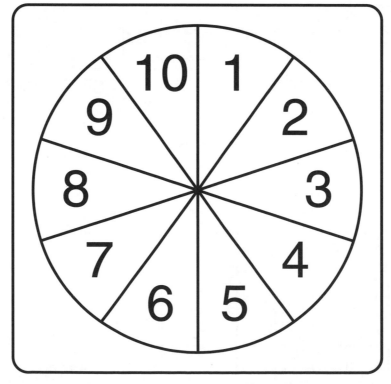

9 to 5 War

Players

This is a card game for two players.

Materials

- one pile per player of 9s and 5s cut from the two *9 to 5 War Cards* Activity Pages in the *Discovery Assignment Book*
- one pile per player of 20 other cards. This can be made from *Digit Cards (0–9)* or from a deck of playing cards with face cards removed (1–10, with aces representing 1s).

Rules

1. Players place their two piles face down in front of them.

2. Each player turns over two cards, one from the 9s and 5s pile, and one from the other pile.

3. Each player should say a number sentence that tells the product of his or her two cards. Whoever has the greater product wins all four cards.

4. If there is a tie, then each player turns over two more cards. The player with the greater product of the second pairs wins all eight cards.

5. Play for ten minutes or until the players run out of cards. The player with more cards at the end is the winner.

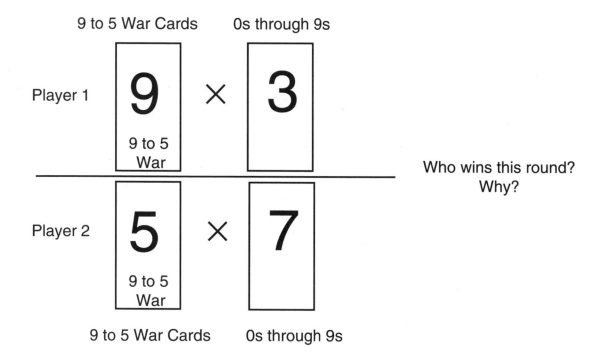

Who wins this round?
Why?

9 to 5 War Cards

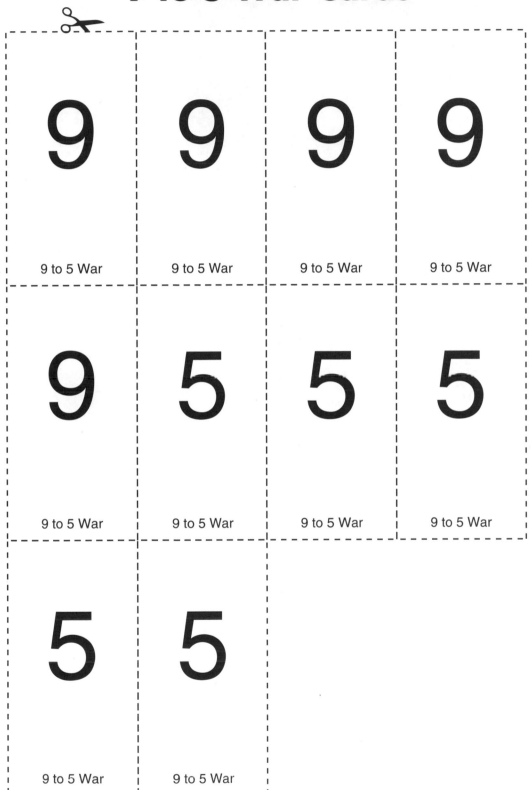

9 to 5 War Cards

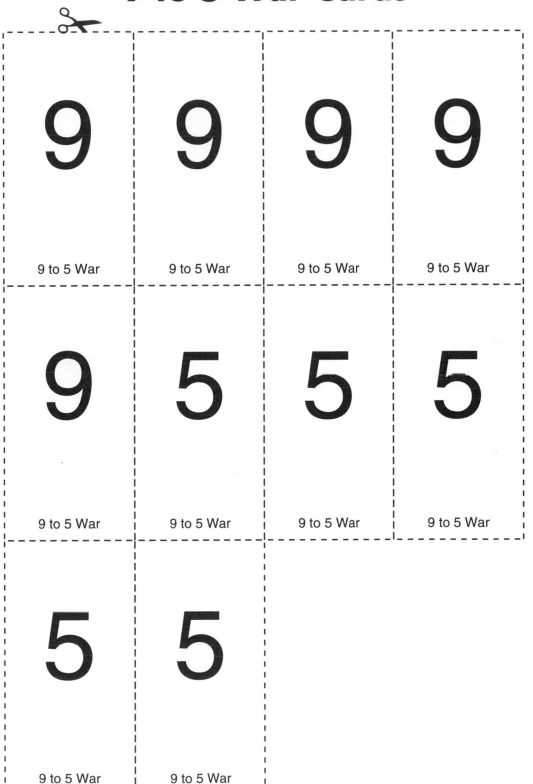

Digit Cards

9   8   7   6

Digit Cards   Digit Cards   Digit Cards   Digit Cards

5   4   3   2

Digit Cards   Digit Cards   Digit Cards   Digit Cards

1   0

Digit Cards   Digit Cards

Digit Cards

9

Digit Cards

8

Digit Cards

7

Digit Cards

6

Digit Cards

5

Digit Cards

4

Digit Cards

3

Digit Cards

2

Digit Cards

1

Digit Cards

0

Digit Cards

Operation Target

Players

This is a cooperative contest for two or three people.

Materials

- paper
- pencil
- calculator

Rules

The goal is to use four digits and four operations $(+, -, \times,$ and $\div)$ to make as many different whole numbers as you can.

You must use each of the four digits just once. You can use operations more than once or not at all. (All division operations must give whole numbers. For example, $9 \div 2 = 4.5$ is not allowed.)

16. Use 9, 5, 2, and 1 and $+, -, \times,$ and $\div$ to make as many whole numbers as you can. For example, $9 + 5 \times 2 - 1 = 18$. List the numbers you make and show how you made them.

    A. What is the largest whole number you can make?

    B. What is the smallest whole number you can make?

    C. How many whole numbers less than 10 can you make? Write number sentences for each number.

    D. What whole numbers can you make in more than one way? Show at least two number sentences for each.

17. Pick four different digits. Make as many whole numbers as you can using your four new digits and $+, -, \times,$ and $\div$. List the numbers you make and show how you made them.

18. Nila used 1, 2, 3, and 4 to make 10. How do you think she did it? Can you think of another way?

19. Luis used 1, 2, 3, and 4 to make 24. How could he have done it?

20. Romesh used 1, 3, 5, and 7 to make 8. How could he have done it?

21. Make up your own problem like those in Questions 18, 19, and 20.

Operation Target

Operation Target is a game that can be played many ways. One set of rules for the game is in Unit 7 Lesson 1. Here is another way to play:

- Use the four digits 1, 4, 6, and 8 and four operations (+, −, ×, and ÷).
- You must use each of the four digits just once.
- You can use each operation more than once or not at all.
- You can make two-digit numbers by putting two digits together. For example, you can use the numbers 14 or 68.
- No operation should give you a fraction, a decimal, or a negative number.

5. Here is a way to make the number 1:
    $4 - 18 \div 6 = ?$ (First divide: $18 \div 6 = 3$)
    $4 - 3 = 1$ (Then subtract 3 from 4.)

    Find another way to make the number 1, following the new rules.

6. Make at least five numbers using these rules.

7. What is the largest number you can make?

8. What is the smallest number you can make?

Challenge: Make all the numbers from 0 to 9.

Mixed-Up Tables

Fill in these multiplication tables:

1.

×	2	4	8
2			
4		16	
8			

2.

×	1	3	9
1			
3			
9			

3. What patterns do you see in the table in Question 1?

4. What patterns do you see in the table in Question 2?

5.

×	10	5	0
10			
5			
0			

6.

×	6	5	7
6			
5			
7			

7. What patterns do you see in the table in Question 5?

8. What patterns do you see in the table in Question 6?

9.

×	8	6	4
8			
6			
4			

10.

×	8	6	3
8			
6			
3			

11.

×	2	5	8
9			
4			
7			

12.

×	7	6	4
3			
9			
10			

Fill in these division tables. Divide the large number across the top by the small number on the side.

13.

Dividend

÷	24	30	36
2			18
3		10	
6			

Divisor

14.

Dividend

÷	16	32	40
2			
4			
8			

Divisor

This section includes the multiplication and division *Triangle Flash Cards* for the 2s, 3s, 5s, 9s, 10s, Square Numbers, Last Six Facts, and *Triangle Flash Cards Masters*. See the Math Facts Calendar in Section 4 for when to use each group of *Triangle Flash Cards*.

To use the flash cards to study the multiplication facts, one partner covers the corner containing the highest number with his or her thumb (this number is lightly shaded). This number will be the answer to a multiplication problem, the product. The second person multiplies the two uncovered numbers, the factors. Partners should take turns quizzing each other on the multiplication facts.

As a student is quizzed, he or she places each flash card into one of three piles: those facts known and answered quickly, those that can be figured out with a strategy, and those that need to be learned. Once students have sorted all their cards, they circle those facts that they know and can answer quickly on a copy of the *Multiplication Facts I Know* chart that can be found in Section 5.

Using the *Triangle Flash Cards* to Study the Multiplication Facts and Update the *Multiplication Facts I Know* Chart

Using the *Triangle Flash Cards* to Study the Division Facts and Update the *Division Facts I Know* Chart

To use the flash cards to study the division facts, one partner covers the number in the square. This number is the answer to the division problem, the quotient. (The number in the circle is the divisor.) The second person solves a division fact using the two uncovered numbers. Partners should take turns quizzing each other on the division facts.

As a student is quizzed, he or she places each flash card into one of three piles: those facts known and answered quickly, those that can be figured out with a strategy, and those that need to be learned. Once students have sorted all their cards, they circle those facts that they know and can answer quickly on a copy of the *Division Facts I Know* chart that can be found in Section 5.

Note that each card represents all four facts in a fact family, for example, 6×4, 4×6, $24 \div 6$, and $24 \div 4$. When students are practicing the multiplication facts, remind them of the turn-around facts. If they know $4 \times 6 = 24$, they also know $6 \times 4 = 24$. They should circle both facts on their *Multiplication Facts I Know* charts.

When students are practicing the division facts, they can go through the cards twice, once by covering the number in the circle and once by covering the number in the square. Alternatively, students can go through the cards once and then give the remaining division fact in the fact family. They should circle both facts on their *Division Facts I Know* charts.

Triangle Flash Cards: 2s

- Work with a partner. Each partner cuts out the flash cards below.
- Your partner chooses one card at a time and covers one corner.
- To quiz you on a multiplication fact, your partner covers the shaded number. Multiply the two uncovered numbers.
- To quiz you on a division fact, your partner covers the number in the square or the number in the circle. Solve a division fact with the two uncovered numbers.
- Divide the cards into three piles: those facts you know and can answer quickly, those you can figure out with a strategy, and those you need to learn.
- Practice the last two piles again. Then make a list of the facts you need to practice at home.
- Repeat the directions for your partner.

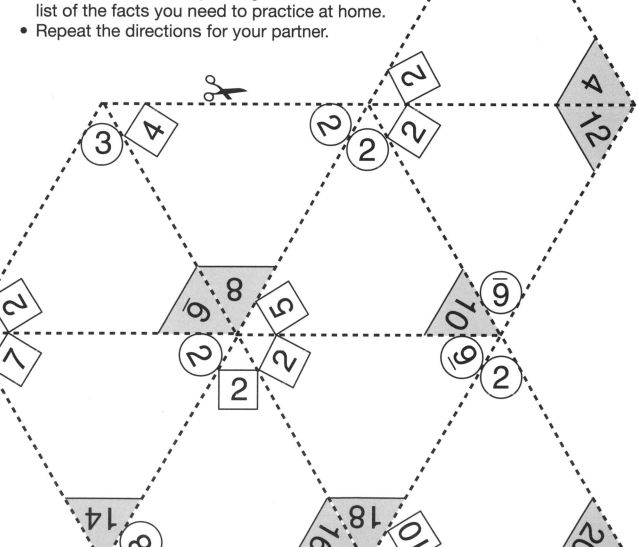

Triangle Flash Cards: 3s

- Work with a partner. Each partner cuts out the flash cards below.
- Your partner chooses one card at a time and covers one corner.
- To quiz you on a multiplication fact, your partner covers the shaded number. Multiply the two uncovered numbers.
- To quiz you on a division fact, your partner covers the number in the square or the number in the circle. Solve a division fact with the two uncovered numbers.
- Divide the cards into three piles: those facts you know and can answer quickly, those you can figure out with a strategy, and those you need to learn.
- Practice the last two piles again. Then make a list of the facts you need to practice at home.
- Repeat the directions for your partner.

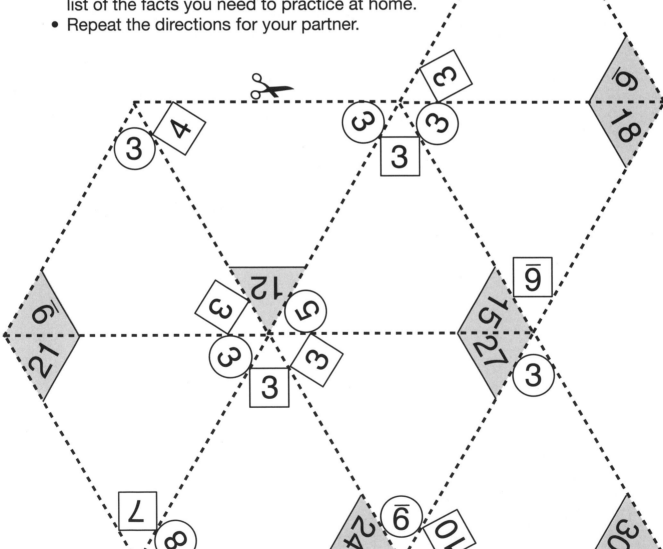

Triangle Flash Cards: 5s

- Work with a partner. Each partner cuts out the flash cards below.
- Your partner chooses one card at a time and covers one corner.
- To quiz you on a multiplication fact, your partner covers the shaded number. Multiply the two uncovered numbers.
- To quiz you on a division fact, your partner covers the number in the square or the number in the circle. Solve a division fact with the two uncovered numbers.
- Divide the cards into three piles: those facts you know and can answer quickly, those you can figure out with a strategy, and those you need to learn.
- Practice the last two piles again. Then make a list of the facts you need to practice at home.
- Repeat the directions for your partner.

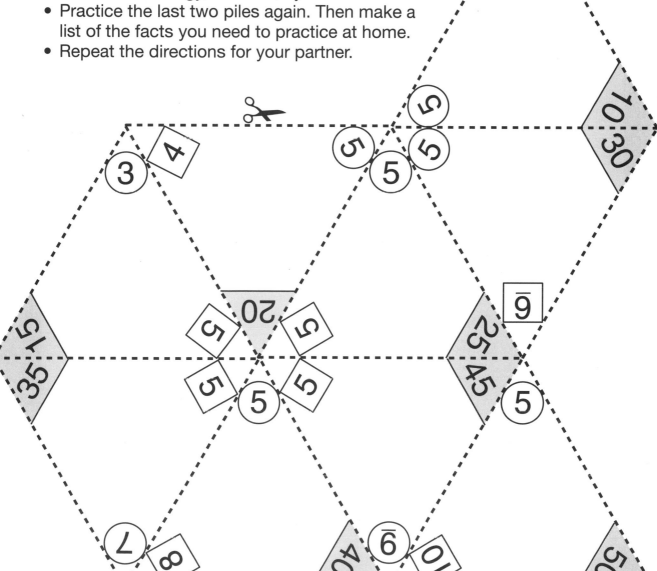

Triangle Flash Cards: 9s

- Work with a partner. Each partner cuts out the flash cards below.
- Your partner chooses one card at a time and covers one corner.
- To quiz you on a multiplication fact, your partner covers the shaded number. Multiply the two uncovered numbers.
- To quiz you on a division fact, your partner covers the number in the square or the number in the circle. Solve a division fact with the two uncovered numbers.
- Divide the cards into three piles: those facts you know and can answer quickly, those you can figure out with a strategy, and those you need to learn.
- Practice the last two piles again. Then make a list of the facts you need to practice at home.
- Repeat the directions for your partner.

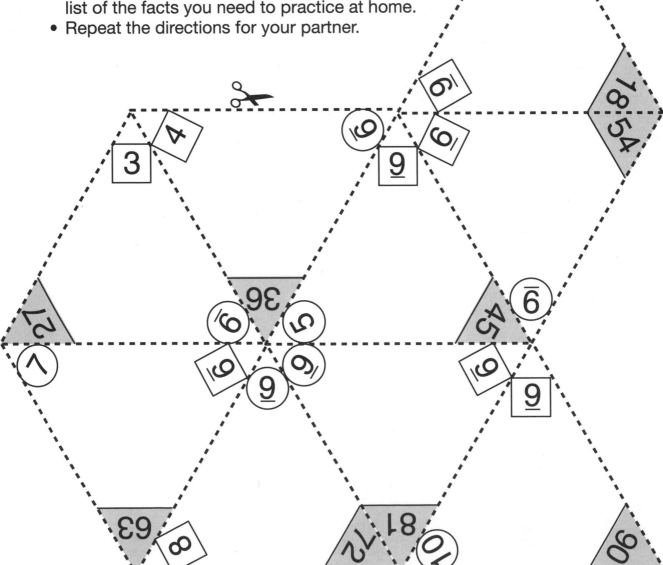

Triangle Flash Cards: 10s

- Work with a partner. Each partner cuts out the flash cards below.
- Your partner chooses one card at a time and covers one corner.
- To quiz you on a multiplication fact, your partner covers the shaded number. Multiply the two uncovered numbers.
- To quiz you on a division fact, your partner covers the number in the square or the number in the circle. Solve a division fact with the two uncovered numbers.
- Divide the cards into three piles: those facts you know and can answer quickly, those you can figure out with a strategy, and those you need to learn.
- Practice the last two piles again. Then make a list of the facts you need to practice at home.
- Repeat the directions for your partner.

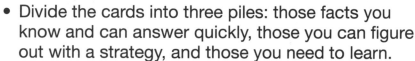

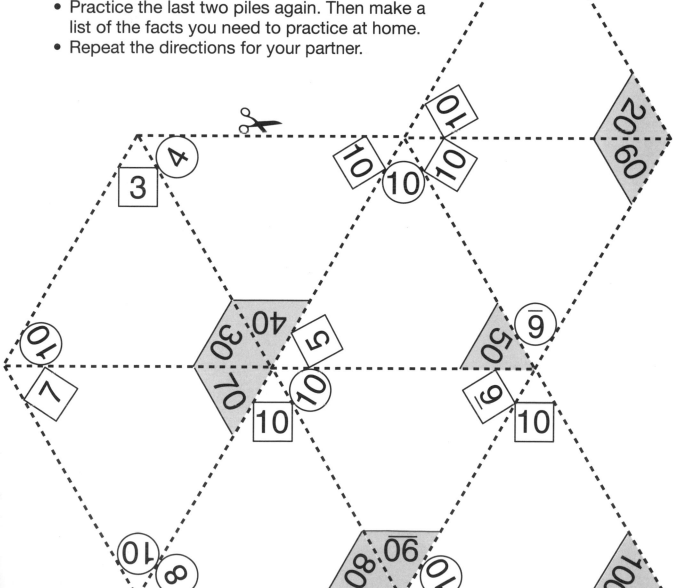

Triangle Flash Cards: Square Numbers

- Work with a partner. Each partner cuts out the flash cards below.
- Your partner chooses one card at a time and covers one corner.
- To quiz you on a multiplication fact, your partner covers the shaded number. Multiply the two uncovered numbers.
- To quiz you on a division fact, your partner covers one of the smaller numbers on each card. Solve a division fact with the two uncovered numbers.
- Divide the cards into three piles: those facts you know and can answer quickly, those you can figure out with a strategy, and those you need to learn.
- Practice the last two piles again. Then make a list of the facts you need to practice at home.
- Repeat the directions for your partner.

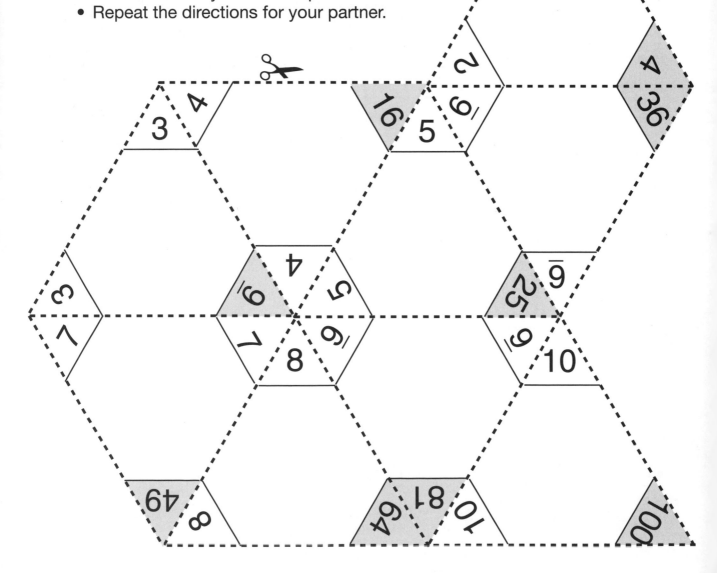

Triangle Flash Cards:
Last Six Facts

- Work with a partner. Each partner cuts out the flash cards below.
- Your partner chooses one card at a time and covers one corner.
- To quiz you on a multiplication fact, your partner covers the shaded number. Multiply the two uncovered numbers.
- To quiz you on a division fact, your partner covers the number in the square or the number in the circle. Solve a division fact with the two uncovered numbers.
- Divide the cards into three piles: those facts you know and can answer quickly, those you can figure out with a strategy, and those you need to learn.
- Practice the last two piles again. Then make a list of the facts you need to practice at home.
- Repeat the directions for your partner.

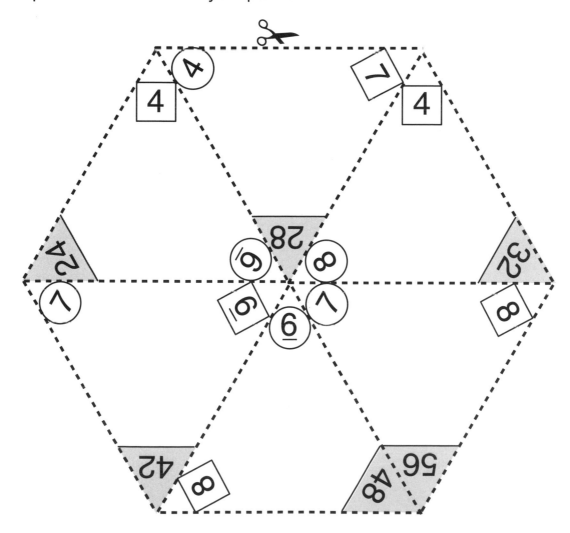

Triangle Flash Card Master

- Make a flash card for each fact that is not circled on your *Multiplication* and *Division Facts I Know* charts. Write the product in the shaded corner of each triangle. Then cut out the flash cards.
- Your partner chooses one card at a time and covers one corner.
- To quiz you on a multiplication fact, your partner covers the shaded number. Multiply the two uncovered numbers.
- To quiz you on a division fact, your partner covers the number in the square or the number in the circle. Solve a division fact with the two uncovered numbers.
- Repeat the directions for your partner.

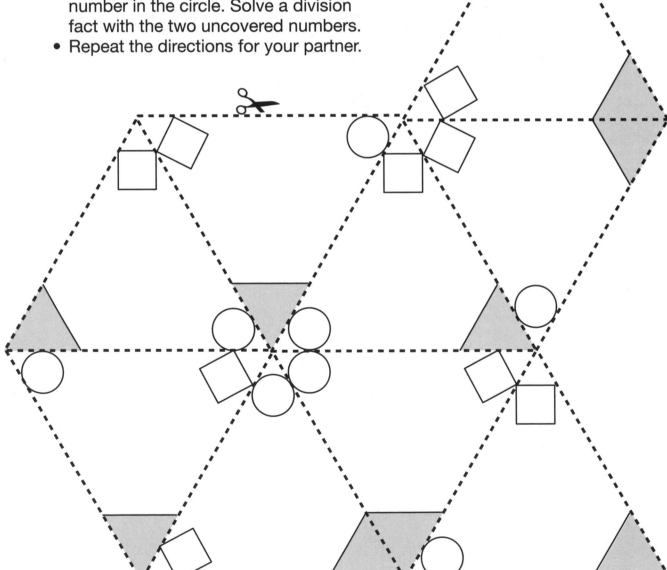

Triangle Flash Card Master

- Make a flash card for each fact that is not circled on your *Multiplication* and *Division Facts I Know* charts. Write the product in the shaded corner of each triangle. Then cut out the flash cards.
- Your partner chooses one card at a time and covers one corner.
- To quiz you on a multiplication fact, your partner covers the shaded number. Multiply the two uncovered numbers.
- To quiz you on a division fact, your partner covers the number in the square or the number in the circle. Solve a division fact with the two uncovered numbers.
- Repeat the directions for your partner.

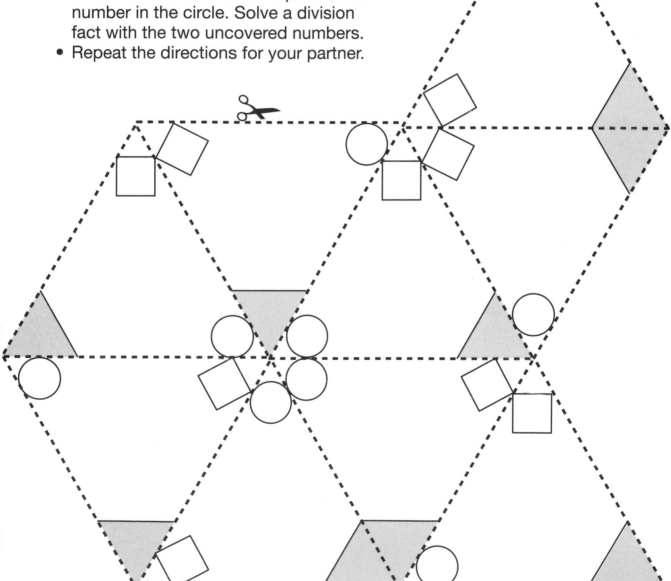

The Addition and Subtraction Math Facts Review contains games and activities that can be used by those students who need extra practice with the addition and subtraction facts. Some of the games and activities are from previous grades of the *Math Trailblazers* curriculum.

Items 1C and 1E in the Daily Practice and Problems for Unit 1 provide addition fact inventory tests. Items 1K and 1O provide subtraction fact inventory tests. Use these tests to see which of your students need more work with the addition and subtraction facts. Those who can find answers quickly and efficiently will continue to practice the addition and subtraction facts throughout the year as they engage in labs, activities, and games, and as they solve problems in the DPP and Home Practice. However, for those students who need extra practice, we have developed games, activities, and flash cards, which can be found in this section.

After you use DPP items 1C, 1E, 1K, and 1O for Unit 1 and have identified students who need extra practice with the addition and subtraction facts, use the diagnostic tests at the end of this section to help you find out which facts these students need to practice. The following table suggests which activities from this section you should assign to students who do not do well on specific diagnostic tests.

Diagnostic Test	Games and Flash Cards
Addition Test: Doubles, 2s, 3s	*Add 1, 2, 3* *Path to Glory* *Path to Glory: 100 Loses* *Path to Glory: Challenge* *Triangle Flash Cards* for Groups A, B, C, D, E
Addition Test: More Addition Facts	*Add 4, 5, 6* *Addition War!* *Mixed-Up Addition Tables 1* and *2* *Line Math 1–5* *Triangle Flash Cards* for Groups C, D, E, F, G
Subtraction Facts: Count-Ups	*Subtract 1, 2, 3: 10* *Triangle Flash Cards* for Groups A, B, C, D
Subtraction Facts: Count-Backs	*Path to Glory: Subtraction* *Subtract 1, 2, 3: 10* *Triangle Flash Cards* for Groups A, B, C, D
Subtraction Facts: Using a Ten	*Subtraction 9 to 5* *Triangle Flash Cards* for Groups E, F, G
Subtraction Facts: Doubles and Others	*Make N: + and −* *Make N: Challenge* *Difference War!* *Triangle Flash Cards* for Groups C, D, E

Students should gradually use the activities, games, and flash cards provided in the Addition and Subtraction Math Facts Review at home with family members. They should concentrate on one small group of facts at a time. Practicing small groups of facts often (for short periods of time) is more effective than practicing many facts less often (for long periods of time). While students practice the addition and subtraction facts at home, in class they should be encouraged to use strategies, calculators, and printed addition and subtraction tables. These tools allow students to continue to develop number sense and work on interesting problems and experiments while they are learning the facts. In this way, students who need extra practice are not prevented from learning more complex mathematics because they do not know all the math facts.

After students have been given the opportunity to use some of the items provided in the Addition and Subtraction Math Facts Review, you can administer the appropriate tests a second time to see students' progress. Alternative forms for each test are located at the end of this section. These tests should be administered over a period of time.

For more information about the distribution of the practice and assessment of the math facts in *Math Trailblazers,* see the TIMS Tutor: *Math Facts* in the *Teacher Implementation Guide.*

Add 1, 2, 3

Players

This is a game for two players.

Rules

1. Player 1 (P1) adds 1, 2, or 3 to 0 and completes the number sentence:
   0 + _____ = _____.

2. Player 2 (P2) adds 1, 2, or 3 to Player 1's answer and records a
   number sentence.

3. Play continues. The player who reaches 10 exactly, wins. A game is
   started for you.

P1: 0 + _2_ = _2_ P2: _2_ + _1_ = _3_ P1: _3_ + _3_ = _6_ P2: _6_ + ____ = ____ P1: ____ + ____ = ____ P2: ____ + ____ = ____ P1: ____ + ____ = ____ P2: ____ + ____ = ____	P1: 0 + ____ = ____ P2: ____ + ____ = ____ P1: ____ + ____ = ____ P2: ____ + ____ = ____ P1: ____ + ____ = ____ P2: ____ + ____ = ____ P1: ____ + ____ = ____ P2: ____ + ____ = ____
P1: 0 + ____ = ____ P2: ____ + ____ = ____ P1: ____ + ____ = ____ P2: ____ + ____ = ____ P1: ____ + ____ = ____ P2: ____ + ____ = ____ P1: ____ + ____ = ____ P2: ____ + ____ = ____	P1: 0 + ____ = ____ P2: ____ + ____ = ____ P1: ____ + ____ = ____ P2: ____ + ____ = ____ P1: ____ + ____ = ____ P2: ____ + ____ = ____ P1: ____ + ____ = ____ P2: ____ + ____ = ____

Path to Glory

Players

This is a game for two players.

Rules

Start at 0. Take turns adding 1, 2, 3, 10, 20, or 30. Write each number you add in a circle. Write the sums in the squares as you go. The player who reaches 100 exactly is the winner.

Here is the beginning of a game:

| 0 |→(+10)→| 10 |→(+20)→| 30 |→

Play 2 or 3 games. Then, write about what happened. Tell how to win.

Path to Glory: 100 Loses

Players

This game is for two players.

Rules

Start at 0. Take turns adding 1, 2, 3, 10, 20, or 30. Write each number you add in a circle. Write the sums in the squares as you go. The player who reaches 100 or more, loses.

Here is the beginning of a game: $\boxed{0}$—$(+1)$→$\boxed{1}$—$(+30)$→$\boxed{31}$→

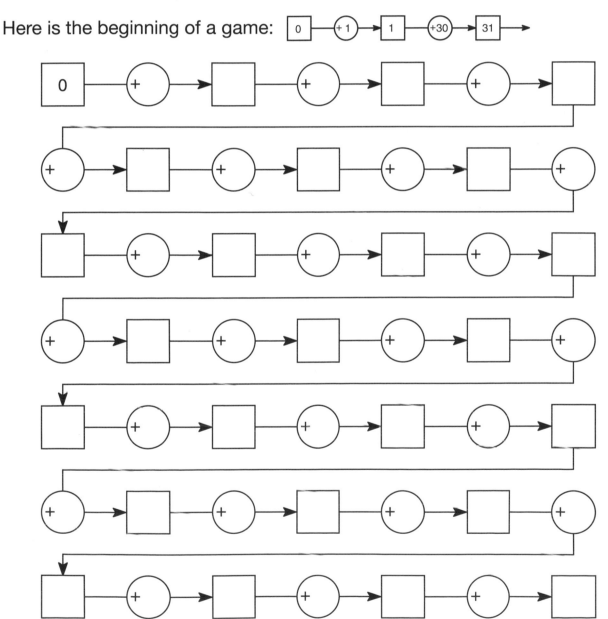

Play 2 or 3 games. Then, write about what happened. Tell how to win.

Path to Glory: Challenge

Players

This is a game for two players.

Rules

Start at 0. Take turns adding 1, 2, 3, 10, 20, or 30. Write each number you add in a circle. Write the sums in the squares as you go. Can you reach 100 in exactly 11 steps?

Is there another way to reach 100 in exactly 11 steps? Write about what happened.

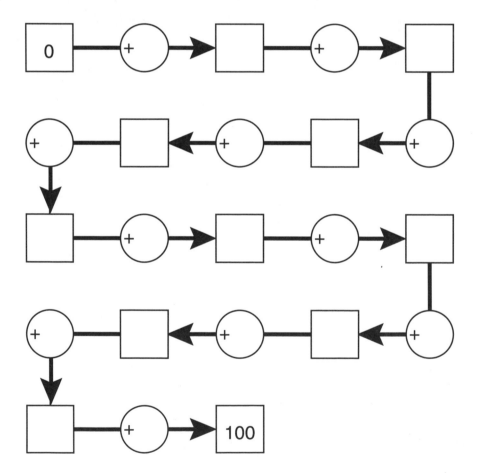

Add 4, 5, 6

Players

This is a game for two players.

Rules

1. Player 1 (P1) adds 4, 5, or 6 to 0 and completes the number sentence:
   0 + _____ = _____.
2. Player 2 (P2) adds 4, 5, or 6 to Player 1's answer and records a number sentence.
3. Play continues. The player who gets to 30 or more, wins. A game is started for you.

P1: 0 + *6* = *6*	P1: 0 + _____ = _____
P2: *6* + *5* = *11*	P2: _____ + _____ = _____
P1: *11* + *4* = *15*	P1: _____ + _____ = _____
P2: *15* + _____ = _____	P2: _____ + _____ = _____
P1: _____ + _____ = _____	P1: _____ + _____ = _____
P2: _____ + _____ = _____	P2: _____ + _____ = _____
P1: _____ + _____ = _____	P1: _____ + _____ = _____
P2: _____ + _____ = _____	P2: _____ + _____ = _____
P1: 0 + _____ = _____	P1: 0 + _____ = _____
P2: _____ + _____ = _____	P2: _____ + _____ = _____
P1: _____ + _____ = _____	P1: _____ + _____ = _____
P2: _____ + _____ = _____	P2: _____ + _____ = _____
P1: _____ + _____ = _____	P1: _____ + _____ = _____
P2: _____ + _____ = _____	P2: _____ + _____ = _____
P1: _____ + _____ = _____	P1: _____ + _____ = _____
P2: _____ + _____ = _____	P2: _____ + _____ = _____

Addition War!

Players

This is a card game for two players.

Materials

You need *Digit Cards* with digits 0 to 9 on them.
You can use *Digit Cards* or regular playing cards. (Let the Ace = 1 and the Jack = 0. Remove the other face cards.)

Rules

1. Deal out all the cards.
2. Each player turns over two cards and says a number sentence that tells the sum of the numbers he or she turned up. Whoever has the larger sum wins all four cards.
3. If there is a tie, turn over two more cards. The larger of the second set takes all eight cards.
4. Play for ten minutes or until one player runs out of cards. The player with the most cards at the end wins.

Variations

- Remove 1s, 2s, and 3s for a harder game.
- Whoever has the *smaller* sum takes the cards.
- Play *Subtraction War!* Whoever has the largest difference wins the cards.
- Play with more than two players.

9 8 7 6

Digit Cards Digit Cards Digit Cards Digit Cards

5 4 3 2

Digit Cards Digit Cards Digit Cards Digit Cards

1 0

Digit Cards Digit Cards

Triangle Flash Cards: Addition and Subtraction

Addition Practice

With a partner, use your *Triangle Flash Cards* to practice the addition or subtraction facts. If you are practicing addition, one partner covers the corner containing the highest number. This number will be the answer to an addition problem. The second person adds the two uncovered numbers.

$9 + 4 = ?$

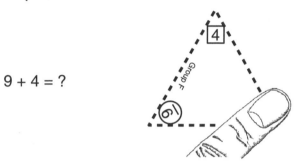

Sorting the Flash Cards

Separate the used cards into three piles: those facts you know and can answer quickly, those you can figure out with a strategy, and those you need to learn. Practice the last two piles again and then make a list of the facts you need to practice at home for homework.

Discuss how you can figure out facts you don't recall at once. Share your strategies with your partner.

Subtraction Practice

If you are practicing subtraction, cover the corner with the square. Subtract the uncovered numbers. Then, go through the cards again, this time covering the number in the circle.

$13 - 9 = ?$

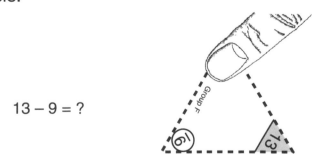

Some subtraction strategies are: counting up, counting back, using a 10, making a 10, using doubles, and using related addition facts.

Triangle Flash Cards:
Group A

1. Cut out the flash cards.

2. Work with a partner. To practice an addition fact, cover the corner with the highest number. (It is shaded.) Add the two uncovered numbers.

3. Divide the cards into three piles: those facts you know and can answer quickly, those you can figure out, and those you need to learn.

4. Practice the last two piles again. Then make a list of the facts you need to practice.

5. To practice a subtraction fact, cover the corner with the square. Subtract the uncovered numbers. Then go through the cards again, this time covering the number in the circle.

6. Repeat the directions in 3 and 4 above each time you go through the cards.

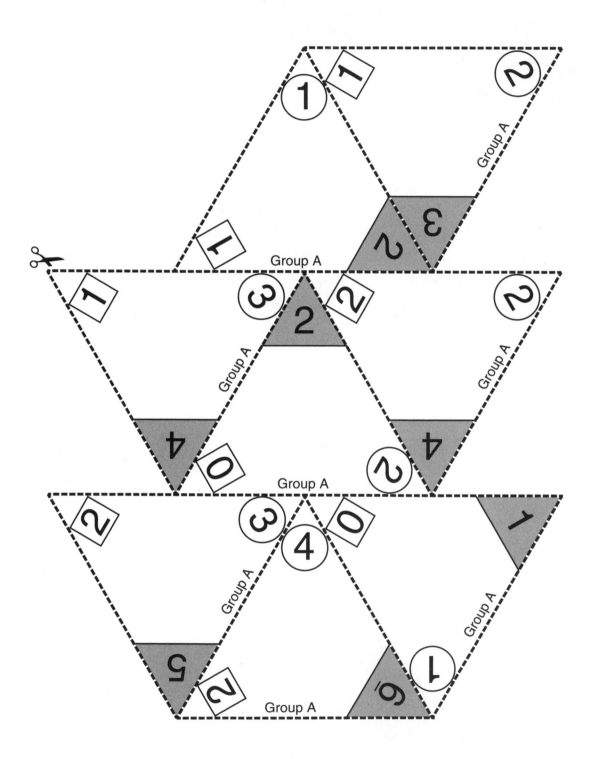

Triangle Flash Cards: Group B

1. Cut out the flash cards.

2. Work with a partner. To practice an addition fact, cover the corner with the highest number. (It is shaded.) Add the two uncovered numbers.

3. Divide the cards into three piles: those facts you know and can answer quickly, those you can figure out, and those you need to learn.

4. Practice the last two piles again. Then make a list of the facts you need to practice.

5. To practice a subtraction fact, cover the corner with the square. Subtract the uncovered numbers. Then go through the cards again, this time covering the number in the circle.

6. Repeat the directions in 3 and 4 above each time you go through the cards.

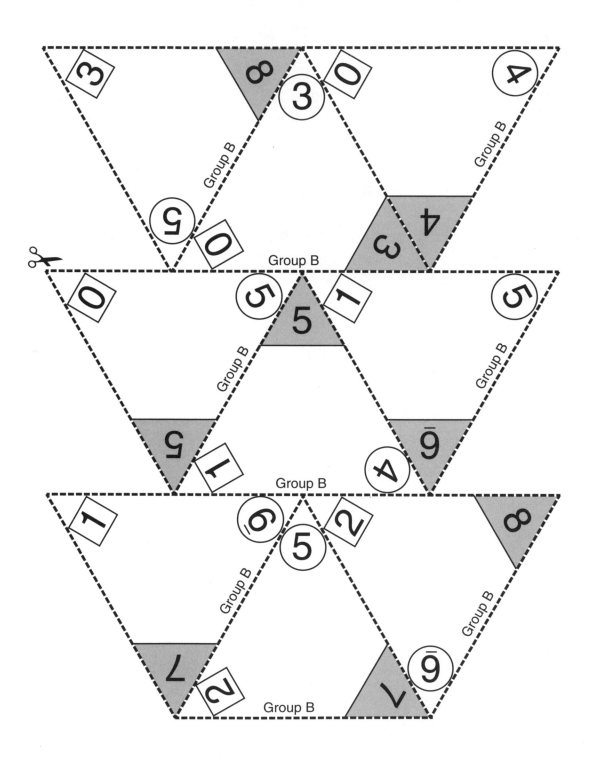

Triangle Flash Cards: Group C

1. Cut out the flash cards.

2. Work with a partner. To practice an addition fact, cover the corner with the highest number. (It is shaded.) Add the two uncovered numbers.

3. Divide the cards into three piles: those facts you know and can answer quickly, those you can figure out, and those you need to learn.

4. Practice the last two piles again. Then make a list of the facts you need to practice.

5. To practice a subtraction fact, cover the corner with the square. Subtract the uncovered numbers. Then go through the cards again, this time covering the number in the circle.

6. Repeat the directions in 3 and 4 above each time you go through the cards.

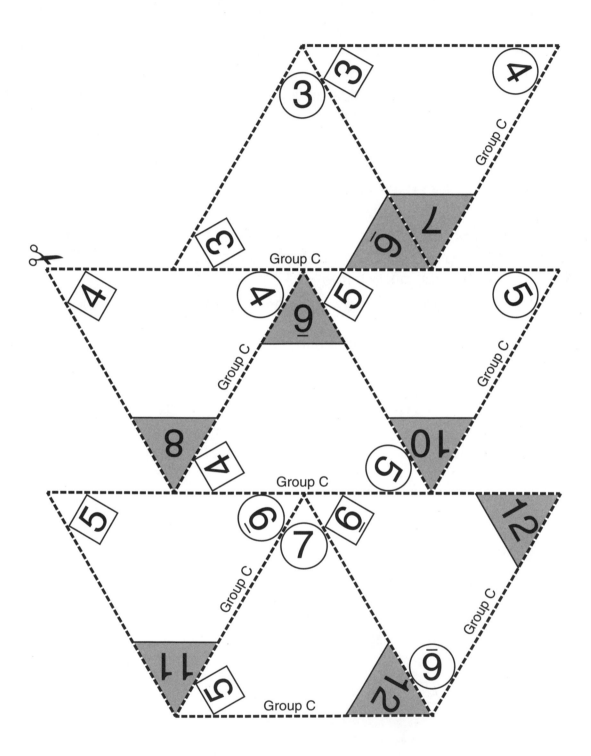

Triangle Flash Cards: Group D

1. Cut out the flash cards.
2. Work with a partner. To practice an addition fact, cover the corner with the highest number. (It is shaded.) Add the two uncovered numbers.
3. Divide the cards into three piles: those facts you know and can answer quickly, those you can figure out, and those you need to learn.
4. Practice the last two piles again. Then make a list of the facts you need to practice.
5. To practice a subtraction fact, cover the corner with the square. Subtract the uncovered numbers. Then go through the cards again, this time covering the number in the circle.
6. Repeat the directions in 3 and 4 above each time you go through the cards.

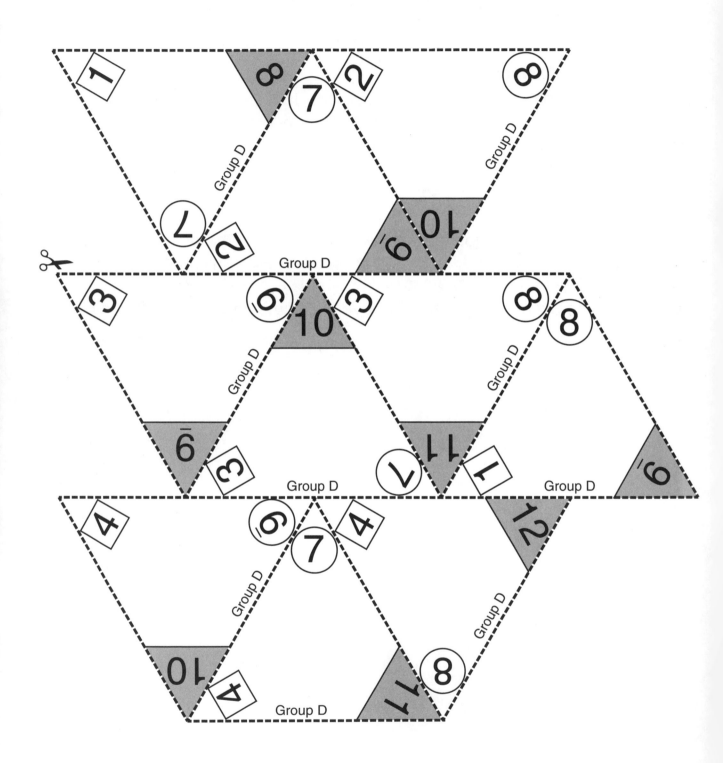

Triangle Flash Cards: Group E

1. Cut out the flash cards.
2. Work with a partner. To practice an addition fact, cover the corner with the highest number. (It is shaded.) Add the two uncovered numbers.
3. Divide the cards into three piles: those facts you know and can answer quickly, those you can figure out, and those you need to learn.
4. Practice the last two piles again. Then make a list of the facts you need to practice.
5. To practice a subtraction fact, cover the corner with the square. Subtract the uncovered numbers. Then go through the cards again, this time covering the number in the circle.
6. Repeat the directions in 3 and 4 above each time you go through the cards.

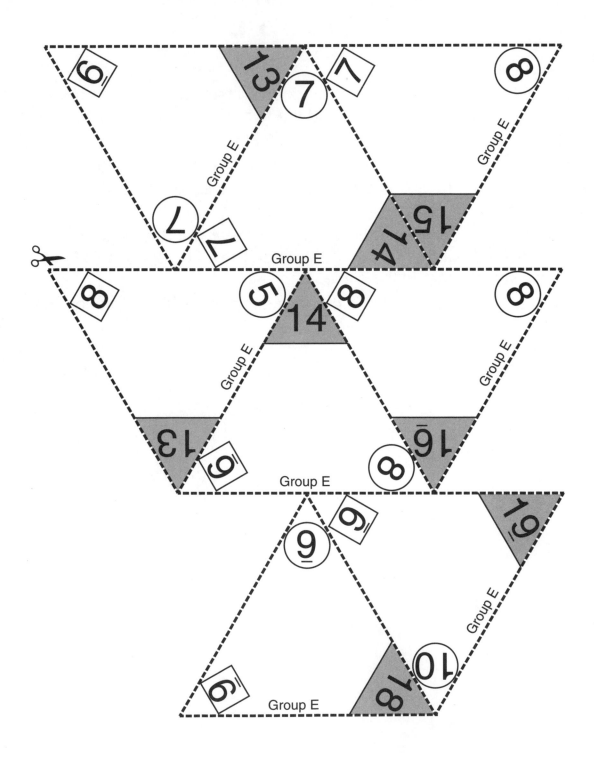

Triangle Flash Cards: Group F

1. Cut out the flash cards.

2. Work with a partner. To practice an addition fact, cover the corner with the highest number. (It is shaded.) Add the two uncovered numbers.

3. Divide the cards into three piles: those facts you know and can answer quickly, those you can figure out, and those you need to learn.

4. Practice the last two piles again. Then make a list of the facts you need to practice.

5. To practice a subtraction fact, cover the corner with the square. Subtract the uncovered numbers. Then go through the cards again, this time covering the number in the circle.

6. Repeat the directions in 3 and 4 above each time you go through the cards.

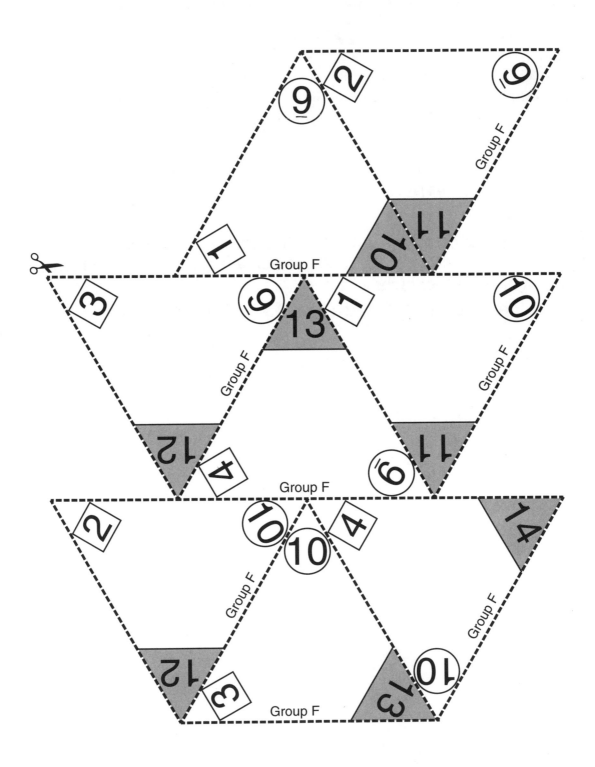

Triangle Flash Cards:
Group G

1. Cut out the flash cards.

2. Work with a partner. To practice an addition fact, cover the corner with the highest number. (It is shaded.) Add the two uncovered numbers.

3. Divide the cards into three piles: those facts you know and can answer quickly, those you can figure out, and those you need to learn.

4. Practice the last two piles again. Then make a list of the facts you need to practice.

5. To practice a subtraction fact, cover the corner with the square. Subtract the uncovered numbers. Then go through the cards again, this time covering the number in the circle.

6. Repeat the directions in 3 and 4 above each time you go through the cards.

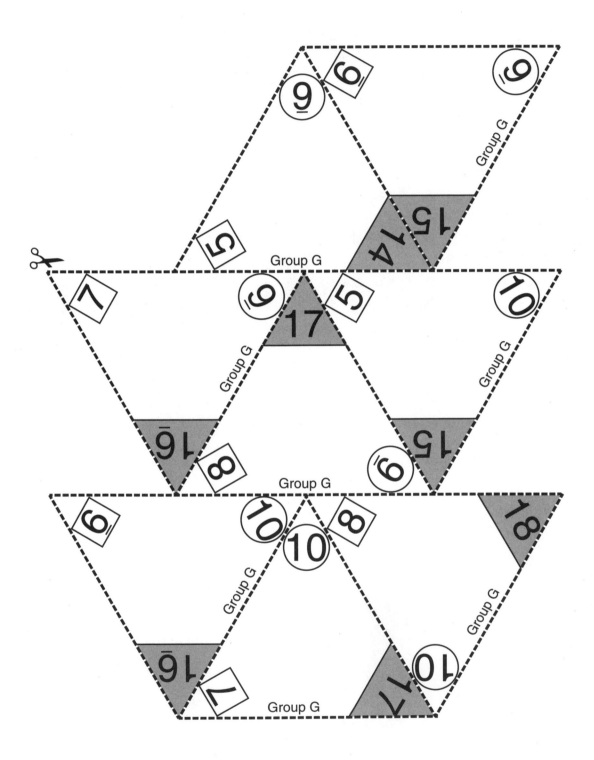

Mixed-Up Addition Table 1

Fill in the missing numbers in these tables.

+	3	6	9	5	7	0
4						
6						
5						
9						
8						
7						

+	5	7	8	2	9	6
7						
3						
5						
4						
8						
9						

Mixed-Up Addition Table 2

Fill in the missing numbers in this table.

+	4	6	2	1	8	7
5						
7						
1						
2						
9						
6						

Put your own numbers along the top and left side of this addition table. Ask a friend to complete the table. Check your friend's work.

+						

Line Math 1

Put 1, 2, 3, 4, and 5 in the boxes so that the sum on each line is 9.
Cut out the digits in the dotted boxes to help.

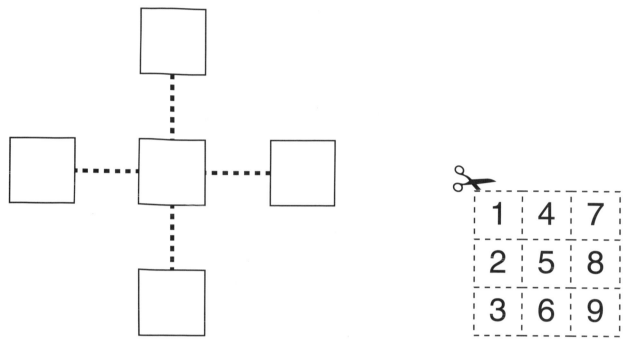

Put 5, 6, 7, 8, and 9 in the boxes so that the sum on each line is 21.

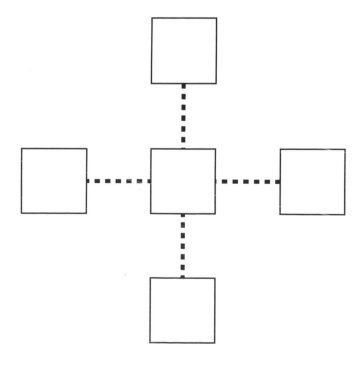

Line Math 2

Put 1, 2, 3, 4, 5, 6, and 7 in the boxes so that the sum on each line is 12. Cut out the digits in the dotted boxes to help.

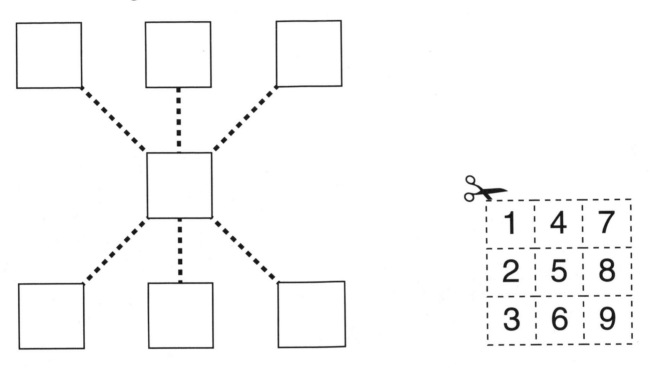

Put 1, 2, 3, 4, 5, and 6 in the boxes so that the sum on each line is 12.

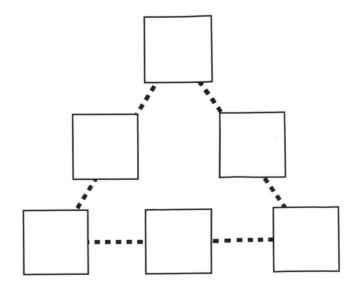

Line Math 3

Put 1, 2, 3, 4, 5, and 6 in the boxes so that the sum on each line is 9.
Cut out the digits in the dotted boxes to help.

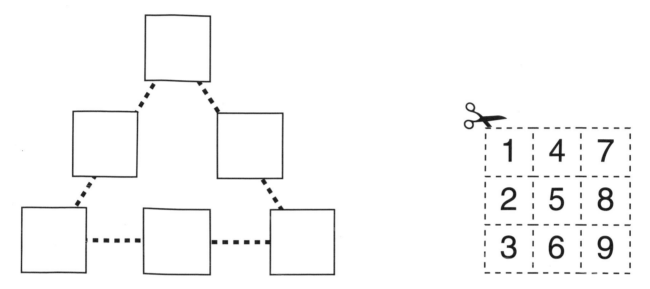

Put 4, 5, 6, 7, 8, and 9 in the boxes so that the sum on each line is 18.

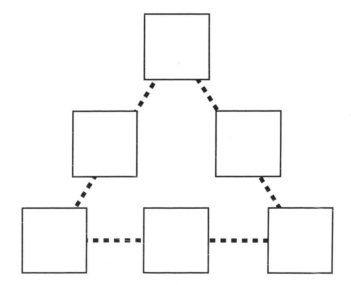

Line Math 4

Put 1, 2, 3, 4, 5, 6, 7, 8, and 9 in the boxes so that the sum on each line is 15. Cut out the digits in the dotted boxes to help.

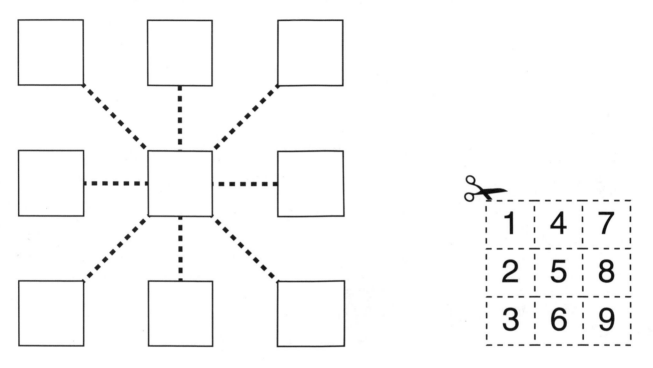

Put 1, 2, 3, 4, 5, 6, 7, 8, and 9 in the boxes so that the sum on each line is 17.

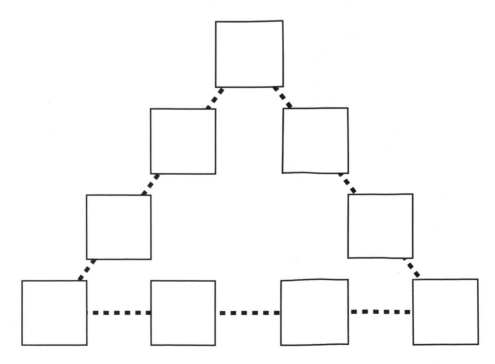

Line Math 5

Put 1, 2, 3, 4, 5, 6, and 7 in the boxes so that the sum on each line is 12. Cut out the digits in the dotted boxes to help.

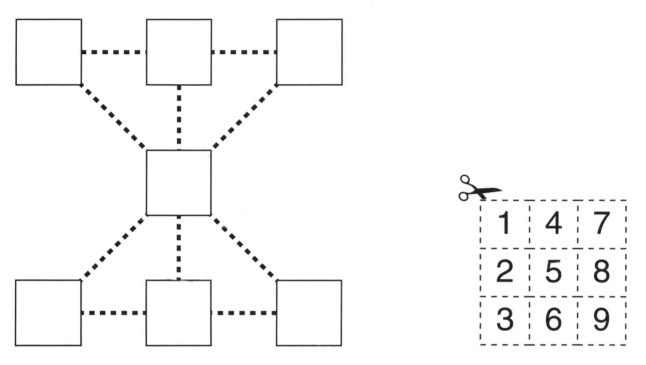

1	4	7
2	5	8
3	6	9

Put 1, 2, 3, 4, 5, 6, 7, 8, and 9 in the boxes so that the sum on each line is 23.

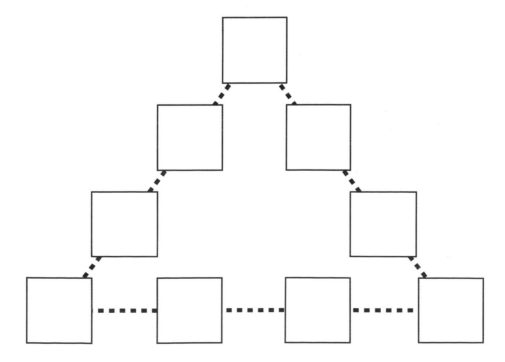

Subtract 1, 2, 3: 10

Players

This is a game for two players.

Rules

1. Player 1 (P1) subtracts 1, 2, or 3 from 10 and completes a number sentence.
2. Player 2 (P2) subtracts 1, 2, or 3 from Player 1's answer and records a sentence.
3. Play continues. The player who reaches 0 exactly, wins. A game is started for you.

P1: 10 − _2_ = _8_

P2: _8_ − _1_ = _7_

P1: _7_ − _3_ = _4_

P2: _4_ − _____ = _____

P1: _____ − _____ = _____

P2: _____ − _____ = _____

P1: _____ − _____ = _____

P2: _____ − _____ = _____

P1: 10 − _____ = _____

P2: _____ − _____ = _____

P1: _____ − _____ = _____

P2: _____ − _____ = _____

P1: _____ − _____ = _____

P2: _____ − _____ = _____

P1: _____ − _____ = _____

P2: _____ − _____ = _____

P1: 10 − _____ = _____

P2: _____ − _____ = _____

P1: _____ − _____ = _____

P2: _____ − _____ = _____

P1: _____ − _____ = _____

P2: _____ − _____ = _____

P1: _____ − _____ = _____

P2: _____ − _____ = _____

P1: 10 − _____ = _____

P2: _____ − _____ = _____

P1: _____ − _____ = _____

P2: _____ − _____ = _____

P1: _____ − _____ = _____

P2: _____ − _____ = _____

P1: _____ − _____ = _____

P2: _____ − _____ = _____

Subtraction 9 to 5

Players

This is a game for two players.

Rules

1. Player 1 (P1) subtracts 9, 8, 7, 6, or 5 from 40 and completes a number sentence.

2. Player 2 (P2) subtracts 9, 8, 7, 6, or 5 from Player 1's answer and records a sentence.

3. Play continues. The player who gets to 4 or less first, wins. A game is started for you.

P1: 40 − _9_ = _31_	P1: 40 − _____ = _____
P2: _31_ − _8_ = _23_	P2: _____ − _____ = _____
P1: _23_ − _6_ = _17_	P1: _____ − _____ = _____
P2: _17_ − _____ = _____	P2: _____ − _____ = _____
P1: _____ − _____ = _____	P1: _____ − _____ = _____
P2: _____ − _____ = _____	P2: _____ − _____ = _____
P1: _____ − _____ = _____	P1: _____ − _____ = _____
P2: _____ − _____ = _____	P2: _____ − _____ = _____

P1: 40 − _____ = _____	P1: 40 − _____ = _____
P2: _____ − _____ = _____	P2: _____ − _____ = _____
P1: _____ − _____ = _____	P1: _____ − _____ = _____
P2: _____ − _____ = _____	P2: _____ − _____ = _____
P1: _____ − _____ = _____	P1: _____ − _____ = _____
P2: _____ − _____ = _____	P2: _____ − _____ = _____
P1: _____ − _____ = _____	P1: _____ − _____ = _____
P2: _____ − _____ = _____	P2: _____ − _____ = _____

Path to Glory: Subtraction

Players

This is a game for two players.

Rules

Start at 100. Take turns subtracting 1, 2, 3, 10, 20, or 30. Write each number you subtract in a circle. Write what remains in the squares as you go. The player who reaches 0 exactly, wins.

Here is the beginning of a game:

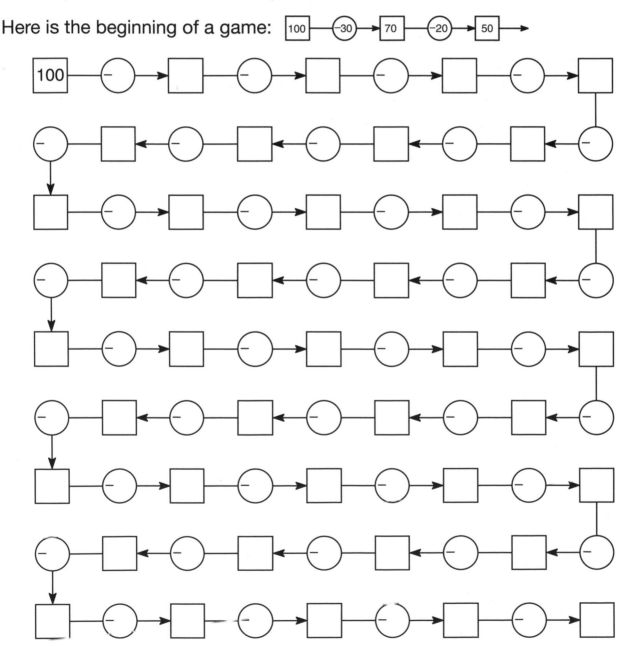

Play 2 or 3 games. Then, write about what happened. Tell how to win.

Make N: + and –

Players

This is an activity for two players.

Materials

You need *Digit Cards* (0, 1, 2, 3, 4, 5, 6, 7, 8, and 9).
You also need *Make N Cards* with the addition sign (+), the subtraction or minus sign (–), the equal sign (=), and the letter *N*.

Rules

1. Work with a partner. Use the cards to make a number sentence for each: *N* = 1, *N* = 2, *N* = 3, . . .
2. Use each digit only once in a number sentence. You can use + and – as often as you like.

   For example, for *N* = 10, one number sentence is $5 + 3 + 2 = N$.

   Another number sentence for *N* = 10 is $N = 6 + 3 + 2 - 1$.
3. Write down your number sentence in the space below. Work in order, starting with *N* = 1.
4. Both players should check that the number sentence is correct.

Use another sheet of paper if you need more room. An example for *N* = 1 is shown. Find another sentence for *N* = 1.

N = 1 $9 - 5 - 3 = N$ _____   *N* = 7 _____

N = 2 _____   *N* = 8 _____

N = 3 _____   *N* = 9 _____

N = 4 _____   *N* = 10 _____

N = 5 _____   *N* = 11 _____

N = 6 _____   *N* = 12 _____

9 8 7 6

Digit Cards   Digit Cards   Digit Cards   Digit Cards

5 4 3 2

Digit Cards   Digit Cards   Digit Cards   Digit Cards

1 0

Digit Cards   Digit Cards

$+$

Make N

$-$

Make N

$+$

Make N

$-$

Make N

N

Make N

N

Make N

$=$

Make N

$=$

Make N

$+$

Make N

$-$

Make N

$+$

Make N

$-$

Make N

Make N: Challenge

Players

This is an activity for two players.

Materials

You need *Digit Cards* (0, 1, 2, 3, 4, 5, 6, 7, 8, and 9).
You also need *Make N Cards* with the addition sign (+), the subtraction or minus sign (−), the equal sign (=), and cards with *N* on them.

Rules

Make N: Challenge is almost the same as *Make N: +* and −. But the goal of this game is to use as many digits as possible.

1. Work with a partner. Use the cards to make a number sentence for each: $N = 1, N = 2, N = 3, \ldots$

2. Use each digit only once in a number sentence. Try to use as many digits as you can. Use + and − as often as you like.

   For example, for $N = 23$, one number sentence is $9 + 8 + 6 = N$.

   But the sentence $9 + 8 + 7 − 6 + 5 = N$ uses more digits, so in this game it's better.

3. Write down your number sentence in the space below. Work in order, starting with $N = 1$.

4. Both players should check that the number sentence is correct.

Use another sheet of paper if you need more room.

$N = 1$ _____ $N = 7$ _____

$N = 2$ _____ $N = 8$ _____

$N = 3$ _____ $N = 9$ _____

$N = 4$ _____ $N = 10$ _____

$N = 5$ _____ $N = 11$ _____

$N = 6$ _____ $N = 12$ _____

Difference War!

Players

This is a card game for two players.

Materials

You need *Difference War Cards* (these have the numbers 7, 8, 9, and 10 on them and a few cards with 5, 6, 11, and 12). You can also make a few cards with your own numbers.

Rules

1. Deal out all the cards.
2. Each player turns over two cards.
3. Each player says or writes a number sentence that tells the difference between the numbers you turn up. Whoever has the greater difference wins all four cards.
4. If there is a tie, turn over two more cards. The greater difference between the second pair takes all eight cards.
5. The player with the most cards at the end wins.

Variations

- Play with all the digits.
- Whoever has the smaller difference takes the cards.
- Play *Addition War!* Whoever has the largest sum wins the cards.

✂

7	8	<u>9</u>	10
Difference War!	Difference War!	Difference War!	Difference War!
7	8	<u>9</u>	10
Difference War!	Difference War!	Difference War!	Difference War!
7	8	<u>9</u>	10
Difference War!	Difference War!	Difference War!	Difference War!

5 6 1112

Difference War! | Difference War! | Difference War! | Difference War!

5 6 1112

Difference War! | Difference War! | Difference War! | Difference War!

Difference War! | Difference War! | Difference War! | Difference War!

Doubles, 2s, 3s

5 + 3 = _____   8 + 8 = _____

7 + 7 = _____   2 + 4 = _____

6 + 3 = _____   6 + 6 = _____

3 + 8 = _____   3 + 3 = _____

9 + 9 = _____   3 + 4 = _____

6 + 2 = _____   7 + 3 = _____

2 + 7 = _____   2 + 8 = _____

5 + 5 = _____   4 + 4 = _____

More Addition Facts

7 + 9 = _____   6 + 8 = _____

4 + 7 = _____   9 + 5 = _____

7 + 6 = _____   8 + 9 = _____

5 + 7 = _____   4 + 6 = _____

7 + 8 = _____   9 + 4 = _____

4 + 5 = _____   8 + 5 = _____

9 + 6 = _____   4 + 8 = _____

6 + 5 = _____   9 + 3 = _____

10 + 4 = _____   9 + 10 = _____

Subtraction Facts: Count-Ups

8 − 6 = _____   10 − 7 = _____

11 − 8 = _____   5 − 3 = _____

9 − 6 = _____   8 − 7 = _____

9 − 7 = _____   7 − 5 = _____

10 − 8 = _____   7 − 6 = _____

6 − 4 = _____   6 − 3 = _____

9 − 5 = _____   6 − 5 = _____

7 − 4 = _____   8 − 5 = _____

Subtraction Facts: Count-Backs

8 – 2 = _____

4 – 3 = _____

9 – 3 = _____

5 – 2 = _____

9 – 2 = _____

11 – 2 = _____

8 – 3 = _____

4 – 2 = _____

9 – 1 = _____

10 – 2 = _____

5 – 0 = _____

10 – 3 = _____

7 – 2 = _____

8 – 1 = _____

11 – 3 = _____

6 – 2 = _____

Subtraction Facts: Using a Ten

17 – 9 = _____   13 – 8 = _____

16 – 7 = _____   13 – 9 = _____

16 – 6 = _____   15 – 7 = _____

17 – 8 = _____   16 – 9 = _____

15 – 10 = _____   12 – 2 = _____

18 – 8 = _____   17 – 10 = _____

15 – 9 = _____   14 – 9 = _____

14 – 4 = _____   13 – 7 = _____

11 – 9 = _____   14 – 8 = _____

Subtraction Facts:
Doubles and Others

11 − 5 = _____   14 − 7 = _____

10 − 4 = _____   12 − 5 = _____

16 − 8 = _____   10 − 5 = _____

15 − 8 = _____   12 − 6 = _____

18 − 9 = _____   11 − 6 = _____

13 − 6 = _____   13 − 5 = _____

12 − 4 = _____   9 − 4 = _____

15 − 6 = _____   11 − 4 = _____